# When
# FOOTBALL *Was*
# FOOTBALL

# ASTON VILLA

© Haynes Publishing, 2011

The right of Graham McColl to be identified as the author of this Work has been asserted
by him in accordance with the Copyright, Designs & Patents Act 1988.

All rights reserved. No part of this publication may be reproduced, stored in a retrieval system
or transmitted, in any form or by any means, electronic, mechanical, photocopying, recording
or otherwise, without prior permission in writing from the publisher.

First published in 2011

A catalogue record for this book is available from the British Library

ISBN: 978-0-857330-47-5


Published by Haynes Publishing, Sparkford, Yeovil,
Somerset BA22 7JJ, UK
Tel: 01963 442030 Fax: 01963 440001
Int. tel: +44 1963 442030 Int. fax: +44 1963 440001
E-mail: sales@haynes.co.uk
Website: www.haynes.co.uk

Haynes North America Inc., 861 Lawrence Drive,
Newbury Park, California 91320, USA

Images © Mirrorpix

Creative Director: Kevin Gardner
Designed for Haynes by BrainWave

Printed and bound in the US

# *When* FOOTBALL *Was* FOOTBALL

# ASTON VILLA

## A Nostalgic Look at a Century of the Club

Graham McColl

# Contents

## Foreword

It was a great honour to have worn the claret and blue of Aston Villa from 1975 to 1985, to have played for a club which had such a great history and to be part of a team that would bring the football club and the fans the greatest prize in club football, the European Cup, which will probably remain as Aston Villa's greatest triumph.

The best way to capture the essence of a football club, especially one with such a rich history as Aston Villa, is through the medium of photography. Photographs capture and store many memories from all eras, and through this book there should be a memory or two for every Villa fan. This book tries to capture what it was like for the fans who stood on the terraces with little room to move, with the elements showering down on them and trying to dampen their spirits, only for one of their heroes to score a goal and send them into delirium. Photographs bring games back to life and show the stories that made the headlines for supporters; I know because as a boy I too was a supporter. I would cut pictures out of the newspaper and place them in a scrapbook to remember the game and if I was lucky I would get the players to autograph them.

Many photographs in this book have never been seen before, which makes it rather unique. Hopefully, when you turn the pages of the book, memories will come flooding back that will enable you to tell a story or two to your friends and fellow fans alike and you can say, "I was there."

Photographs record the good and the bad of football. Who remembers the Saturday when Glasgow Rangers supporters ran riot at Villa Park? Or the pictures next day after an evening game against Liverpool when we won 5-1, with all our goals coming in the first half before some of the Liverpool fans had taken their seats? Or, facing Liverpool once again, in our Championship season, when we won 2-0 and I scored one of the goals?

The good photographer captures the moment for us all in the click of the shutter, sometimes capturing many photographs in a split second. This book aims to bring to you the best and sharpest photographs of your club – pictures that will remind you of how football was before the days of the Premier League.

You will see here a photograph of me holding up the European Cup – my greatest football memory. I hope there is a photograph somewhere for you in this book that brings back a memorable moment.

**Dennis Mortimer**

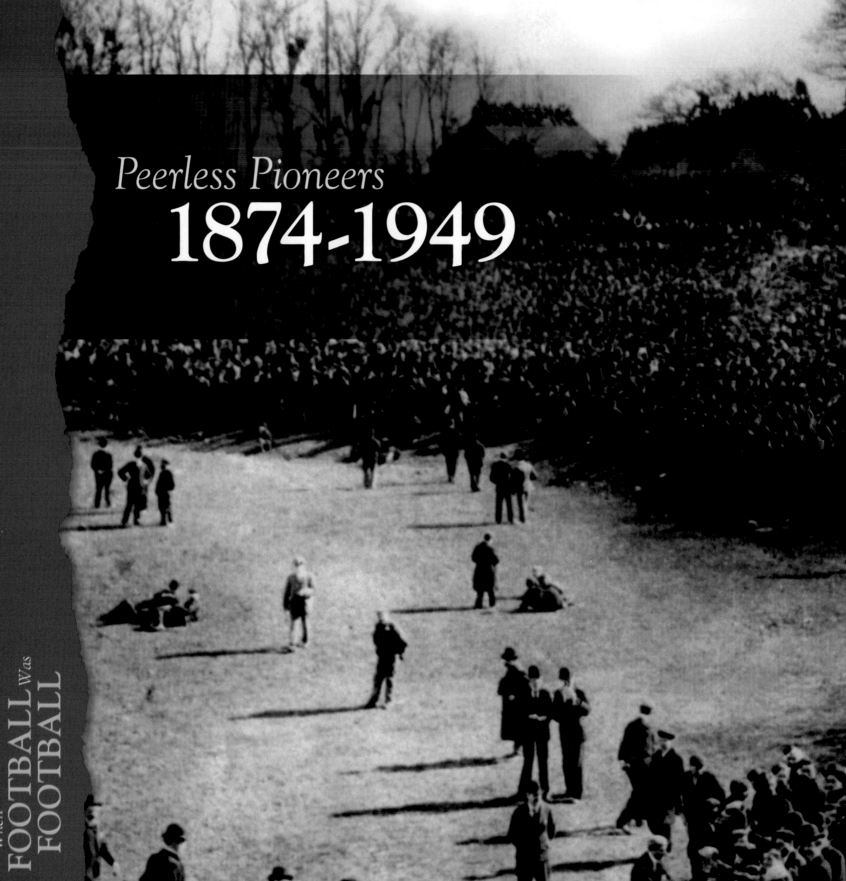

*Peerless Pioneers*
# 1874-1949

Supporters seize every available viewing position for the 1905 FA Cup final between Aston Villa and Newcastle United at the Crystal Palace, South London. The recorded crowd of 101,117 was the first time a six-figure attendance had been registered for a final not involving one of the London clubs. Villa won 2-0 thanks to a brace from Harry Hampton, the centre-forward who had also scored five times en route to the final.

" *I helped to plant the seed and I have seen a strong oak grow.*

George Ramsay, team captain and then secretary-manager during Aston Villa's first five decades "

1874 Members of Villa Cross Wesleyan Chapel form Aston Villa Football Club and contest their first match in March 1875. 1886 A 13-0 FA Cup triumph over Wednesbury Old Athletic establishes Villa's record margin of victory. 1887 Goals from Dennis Hodgetts and Archie Hunter give Villa a 2-0 win over West Bromwich Albion in the FA Cup final as Villa take the trophy for the first time. 1888 At the instigation of William McGregor, an Aston Villa committee man, the Football League is formed. 1894 A 6-3 win at Burnley sees Villa crowned League Champions for the first time. 1895 Villa defeat West Brom 1-0 in the FA Cup final at the Crystal Palace. 1897 Villa successfully defend the league title they had won in 1896 and defeat Everton 3-2 in the FA Cup final to become only the second club to win the double. Villa move to their new home at Aston Lower Grounds, which will eventually become known as Villa Park. 1899 A 5-0 defeat of Liverpool in the final match and title decider takes the League Championship trophy to Villa Park rather than Merseyside. 1900 A record 50,000 Villa Park crowd watch Villa draw 1-1 with closest rivals Sheffield United en route to retaining the title. 1905 Harry Hampton scores twice as Villa beat Newcastle United 2-0 in the FA Cup final. 1910 A record-equalling total of 53 points makes Villa champions of the Football League for a record sixth time. 1913 A new record attendance for an FA Cup final, 120,081, sees Villa win the trophy for a fifth time by beating Sunderland 2-0. 1920 Villa beat Huddersfield Town 1-0 at Stamford Bridge to clinch the first postwar FA Cup. 1933 Billy Walker retires after 13 years with Villa and having scored a club record of 244 goals. 1936 Villa suffer relegation for the first time. 1944 In a two-legged final Villa defeat Blackpool to win the Football League Cup (North), a wartime competition. 1946 The record attendance for Villa Park is set when 76,588 watch Villa take on Derby County in an FA Cup quarter-final.

Andy Ducat, Aston Villa captain, shakes hands with Fred Bullock of Huddersfield Town, prior to the FA Cup final at Stamford Bridge in April 1920. This was Villa's seventh appearance in the final, a then unmatched record.

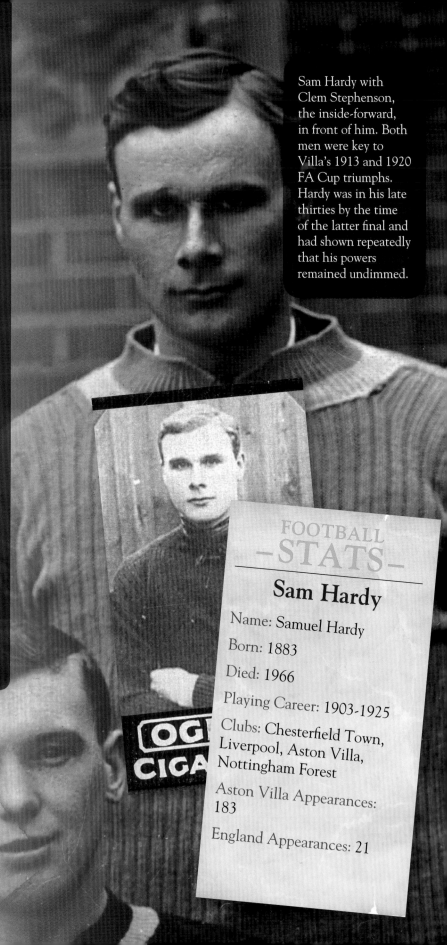

# –LEGENDS–

## Sam Hardy

The departure of Billy George, Aston Villa's first great, long-serving goalkeeper, in 1911, appeared to leave a sizeable vacuum at the club, but Sam Hardy filled it almost immediately. Hardy, who joined Villa from Liverpool in 1912, was nicknamed "Safe and Steady Sam" and his superb powers of anticipation and his unflappable nature made him one of the best goalkeepers England has ever produced. Either side of the First World War, he was the man in goal to keep a clean sheet for Villa in the club's FA Cup final wins in 1913 and 1920.

During the first of those FA Cup victories, Hardy was forced to leave the field following a collision with Harry Martin, the Sunderland winger. Sunderland peppered the Villa goal to try to take advantage, and only luck kept them out before Hardy returned after an eight-minute absence, his leg heavily bandaged, ready to resume his successful repulsion of the Sunderland forward line. During the run to the 1920 final, Hardy and Frank Barson, the Villa centre-half, took a seven-mile detour through country fields to catch a train to Manchester for a tie at Old Trafford after having missed their scheduled connection. Hardy left Villa in 1921, after having refused to accept the Villa committee's rule that players should live in Birmingham – and this time Villa really had a goalkeeping vacuum that they would struggle to fill.

Sam Hardy with Clem Stephenson, the inside-forward, in front of him. Both men were key to Villa's 1913 and 1920 FA Cup triumphs. Hardy was in his late thirties by the time of the latter final and had shown repeatedly that his powers remained undimmed.

*One of the greatest goalkeepers I ever saw.*

Jesse Pennington, England full-back

### FOOTBALL –STATS–

**Sam Hardy**

Name: Samuel Hardy

Born: 1883

Died: 1966

Playing Career: 1903-1925

Clubs: Chesterfield Town, Liverpool, Aston Villa, Nottingham Forest

Aston Villa Appearances: 183

England Appearances: 21

# –LEGENDS–

## Frank Barson

The fearsome figure of centre-half Frank Barson struck terror into opposing forwards and helped keep Aston Villa fundamentally secure and lodged in the top half of the top flight during the early 1920s. His arrival from Barnsley for a British record fee of £2,700 was vital in shoring up a Villa defence that had previously been leaking goals. Barson helped Villa win the FA Cup in the spring of 1920 through adding an edge to the team. At six feet tall and weighing in at 13 stone, Barson was an abrasive player whose broken nose bore testimony to how much he liked a good brawl – his rugged style regularly brought about complaints, from opponents to referees.

The other, less-trumpeted qualities of a man who was a blacksmith by trade were equally important to Villa. He was a good talker who provided much encouragement to his team-mates, close to unbeatable in the air and his passes out of defence were, according to Villa forward Billy Walker, "real beauties". Sadly, despite his influence on the club, Frank was allowed to leave in 1922 for Manchester United. The Villa committee had a residential rule of which Frank, living in Sheffield, fell foul, and Villa's loss was United's gain.

Frank Barson, despite his hard-as-nails reputation, was always good at nurturing young Aston Villa players when he was on the playing staff and he would return to the club as youth coach in 1935, before quickly being promoted to head coach, a role he held until the outbreak of the Second World War.

## FOOTBALL STATS

### Frank Barson

Name: Francis Barson

Born: 1891

Died: 1968

Playing Career: 1911-1931

Clubs: Barnsley, Aston Villa, Manchester United, Watford, Hartlepools United, Wigan Borough, Rhyl Athletic

Aston Villa Appearances: 108

Aston Villa Goals: 10

England Appearances: 1

Goals: 0

> "A man who could not play with Frank Barson behind him would be a very poor fish indeed."
>
> Billy Walker

# Record-Beaters

Prince Henry presents the Aston Villa players with their FA Cup winner's medals after the 1920 final, which had been the first to go to extra-time and which resulted in a 1-0 victory for Villa, who took the Cup to Villa Park for a record sixth time. The goal came 10 minutes into the additional period: Tom Wilson, the Huddersfield centre-half, and Billy Kirton, the Villa inside-right, jumped together for the ball at a Villa corner and the ball ended up in the net. Even some of Wilson's team-mates were sure it was an own goal but Jack "Jimmy" Howcroft, the referee, awarded the goal to Kirton. Howcroft, the best respected and most effective referee of the time, was rarely incorrect.

> *Perhaps we were a bit lucky in regard to the winning goal, but to the end of my life I shall always maintain that on the play we deserved the Cup and the medals.*
> *It was a happy day for all of us.*
>
> Billy Walker, Aston Villa centre-forward

This had been the first Cup final for five years and the first since the conclusion of the First World War. It provided Villa with an opportunity to show that their prewar distinction could continue into the postwar era.

# A Popular Attraction

A back page of the *Daily Mirror* shows a section of the densely packed crowd of almost 75,000 that rolled up at Villa Park on 25th January 1930 to see Villa defeat Walsall 3-1 in their FA Cup tie through two goals from Billy Walker and one from George Brown. Villa had been drawn away but the tie was switched to Villa Park at the request of the Walsall directors.

THE DAILY MIRROR, Monday, January 27, 1930.

Wilfred in Disgrace: See page 12

# Daily Mirror

## ASTON VILLA WIN THEIR CUP-TIE BUT BIRMINGHAM PLAY AGAIN

A small section of the huge crowd of 74,000 at Villa Park, where Aston Villa, playing in rather disappointing form, defeated Walsall by 3—1.

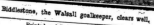

Biddlestone, the Walsall goalkeeper, clears well.

Hibbs, Birmingham goalie, saving against Arsenal, who drew 2—2 at Highbury.—("Daily Mirror" photographs.)

Printed and Published by THE DAILY MIRROR NEWSPAPERS, LTD., at Geraldine House, Rolls Bldgs., Fetter-lane, London, E.C.4.—Monday, January 27, 1930.—Tel. Holborn 4321.

Jimmy McMullan became, in May 1934, the first manager of Aston Villa. Prior to his arrival, the team had been selected by committee although in the first four decades of the club's existence George Ramsay, as secretary-manager, had been a hugely influential figure in the running of the team.

LEFT: McMullan had been a highly talented half-back for Manchester City and Scotland, and captain of both club and country. During the 1933/4 season, his first in football management, he had improved Oldham Athletic's standing to ninth place in the Second Division. He would spend only 17 months in the Villa job, departing on the final Saturday of October 1935 with the club in a state of some turbulence and heading for the first relegation in its history.

15

# Golden Goals

LEFT: Fred Biddlestone, Aston Villa goalkeeper, clears from Hughie Gallacher, the Chelsea forward, during a 6-3 Villa victory at Stamford Bridge in the autumn of 1931. Hitting six was not unusual for Villa – they had done so three times during the previous league season when they had also hit seven in one game and eight in another and had scored 128 league goals, a record for the top flight in England. The early 1930s was something of a golden period for the Villa. They twice came close to landing the league title – in 1931 and 1933 – being pipped narrowly by Arsenal on both occasions; and in this 1931/2 season finished fifth. Not only did they push for prizes but this Villa side was a hugely entertaining one, and although the early 1930s failed to yield any trophies, the Villa support still felt largely satisfied with what was served up for them.

17

# –LEGENDS–

## Pongo Waring

A poor performance from Aston Villa marked the team's visit to Old Trafford on the opening day of the 1930/1 season. The passing was dreadful and after only two minutes the defence conceded the first of three goals to Manchester United. Only one Villa player managed to score, but that man was Pongo Waring, and he hit the United net no fewer than four times as Villa, despite their lack of substance on the day, ran out 4-3 victors. Those four goals would be followed by 46 more from Waring that season, making him the highest-scoring Villa player over a single season and bulking out the record 128 that Villa scored overall in the 1930/1 campaign.

Waring could score all sorts of goals, as might be expected of a man with such a record. He was wonderfully acrobatic in the air, had quick reflexes and was too powerful and strong for most defenders. He rarely left the field at the end of a game without adding to his tally and his goals pushed Villa agonizingly close to the league title in the late 1920s and early 1930s. When not playing football, Pongo was reputedly disorganized and happy-go-lucky – he "clowned his way through life", according to Billy Walker, his equally prolific goalscoring team-mate. On the football field, though, British football has rarely seen a more single-minded and efficient individual than Pongo Waring.

Tom "Pongo" Waring in January 1929, just under a year after his arrival at Aston Villa from Tranmere Rovers and in the midst of a first full season at Villa Park that would see him notch 32 goals, a modest total in comparison with his later goalscoring feats. The "Pongo" nickname was most probably derived from "Pongo the Pup", a 1920s British cartoon character.

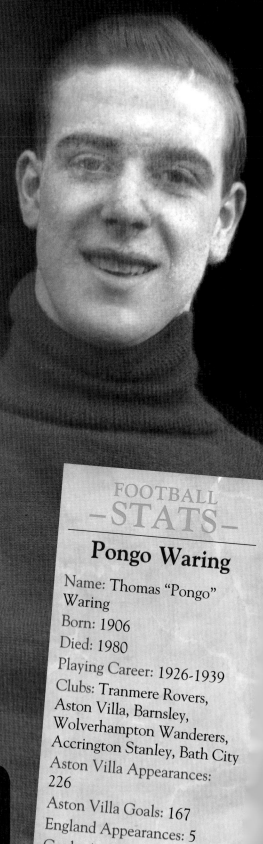

## FOOTBALL –STATS–

### Pongo Waring

Name: Thomas "Pongo" Waring
Born: 1906
Died: 1980
Playing Career: 1926-1939
Clubs: Tranmere Rovers, Aston Villa, Barnsley, Wolverhampton Wanderers, Accrington Stanley, Bath City
Aston Villa Appearances: 226
Aston Villa Goals: 167
England Appearances: 5
Goals: 4

> *There were no rules for Pongo but as captain I think I can claim to have been the only person able to handle him.*
>
> Billy Walker

## THE DAILY MIRROR

Tuesday, January 23, 1934

Page 26

### STERN WARNING TO THE VILLA

#### F.A. ORDER CLUB TO CAUTION

##### CROWDS BY POSTING BILLS

**Waring Suspended for Six Weeks—Who Will Be Arsenal's New Manager?**

By Rex Campbell

The F.A. have issued a stern warning to Aston Villa in connection with the incidents which took place on January 6 at Villa Park during the match against Tottenham Hotspur. The club's chairman, Waring, who was sent off, has been suspended for six weeks.

Aston Villa have been instructed to post bills warning spectators that should there be a recurrence of misconduct the F.A. will be compelled to take further action.

It will be recalled that after the referee had ordered Waring off, missiles, including bottles, were thrown off the field, and so ugly did the situation appear that police patrolled the touchline until the end of the game.

*[remaining column text largely illegible]*

#### BRILLIANT VETERANS

#### LOOKING OUT FOR TALENT

Waring.

#### STADIUM CLUB UPROAR

Kid Berg's Brother Disqualified in a "Come-Back" Fight

#### LEADING GOAL-SCORERS

Glover and Lythgoe Head List—Four Ahead of Nearest Rival

#### DISTANCE TEST FOR GIRL

#### DIVISION III CUP MATCHES

Rival goalkeepers. Ball (taller) and Wall, photographed before a schools competition game for the Woodcock shield at the Bristol City football ground.

### HARVEY STARTS TRAINING

**Tactics He and Gains Must Try to Avoid**

#### REFEREE'S JOB

BY OUR BOXING CORRESPONDENT

#### SPOIL-SPORT TACTICS

#### TWO "LAST WARNINGS"

#### GOLF STAR ON HOLIDAY

Miss Kathleen Garnham, of Walton-on-Naze, who won the French Ladies' open title and the Essex championship last year, is leaving for America on a golfing holiday.

#### THE OPTIMISTS

### Globe-Trotting Greyhound

**17,000 MILES—AND MAY RACE AGAIN**

#### ICE CHAMPIONS BEATEN

#### RIVALS TRAIN TOGETHER!

#### SECOND SPEED LEAGUE

#### AMBITIOUS DIVING PLANS

#### RUGBY PLAYER'S ACCIDENT

The *Daily Mirror* reports a six-week suspension for Pongo Waring after his dismissal in Villa's 5-1 home defeat to Tottenham Hotspur in early January 1934. Some Villa supporters were so incensed by the referee's decision to send off Pongo that they threw missiles on to the playing surface and so, in addition to Waring's suspension, the club was warned of further repercussions if a similar episode were to occur. Pongo would play only three more matches in the remainder of that 1933/4 season, and after six glorious, goalscoring years, his star was firmly on the wane. He would leave Villa in the autumn of 1935, having scored, following his suspension, only 19 further goals, a modest return by his standards.

Danny Blair, Villa full-back, sporting Villa's away kit, looks to close down Pat Beasley of Arsenal during a match at Highbury in March 1934, which ended in a 3-2 win for Arsenal. Villa had been Arsenal's most consistent challengers for the league title in the early 1930s – the previous season Villa had finished only four points behind the champions – but in 1934 they would finish in the lower half of the First Division for the first time in

# –LEGENDS– Billy Walker

If George Walker had had his way, Aston Villa would have been deprived of one of the greatest individuals ever to wear the claret and blue. George, Billy Walker's father, had been a player with Wolverhampton Wanderers and did not wish his son to enter the professional game. But Billy was determined to do so, and at the age of 18 joined Villa. His subsequent scoring feats are all the more remarkable given that he did not make his first-team debut until he was 22 years old. He wasted no time when he did so, scoring a goal in each half as Villa defeated Queen's Park Rangers 2-1 in a home FA Cup tie in January 1920. He had been fielded, to his enormous surprise, at centre-forward, a position he had not played since schooldays, because of Villa's dire injury situation, but, helped by advice from his dad, he quickly adjusted to first-team football and his new role.

During the following 13 years, Billy would add a further 242 goals to that initial brace, securing his place in Villa lore as the most proficient goalscorer the club has ever had on its books. Lithe and quick, with exceptional control and anticipation, and a superb header of the ball, Billy helped make the interwar years hugely enjoyable for Villa followers even if, trophy-wise, the team was unable to add to the 1920 FA Cup triumph that those early Walker goals against QPR had helped to spark. Among his 18 England caps in a 12-year stretch with the national team was an appearance against Scotland at Villa Park in 1922. After Billy left Villa in late 1933, it was not coincidental that the club swiftly went into a dramatic downward spiral.

## FOOTBALL –STATS–

### Billy Walker

Name: William Henry Walker

Born: 1897

Died: 1964

Playing Career: 1920-1933

Clubs: Aston Villa

Aston Villa Appearances: 531

Aston Villa Goals: 244

England Appearances: 18

Goals: 9

Prince Henry shakes hands with Billy Walker as the Aston Villa players line up to meet royalty before the 1920 FA Cup final at Stamford Bridge.

> *His artistry was superb; his skill in ball control unsurpassed. No player was more likely to head the ball into the net than he.*

Villa News & Record on Billy Walker's retirement as a player

ABOVE: Billy Walker (right), now aged 62, leads Nottingham Forest out at Wembley for the 1959 FA Cup final with Luton Town.

ABOVE: Billy Walker, centre, pointing, not long after his departure from Villa. He is here, as manager of Sheffield Wednesday, on the pitch with his team at Wembley, on the day prior to the 1935 FA Cup final, in which they would face West Bromwich Albion. Walker, at 37, was not much older than most of his players, having taken over at Wednesday only 16 months previously. It was quite a feat for such a young and largely untested manager to have taken his team to the FA Cup final in his first full season as a manager. Not only that but Wednesday won, 4-2. Only a decade previously, Walker had trod the same turf in Villa's 1-0 defeat to Newcastle United in the final. Perhaps Billy is pointing out some of his feats on that day or how, also in 1924, he became the first Englishman to score at the stadium, in a match with Scotland.

# Handling the Big Occasion

George Edwards, a forward who joined Aston Villa shortly before the Second World War, shows off some silky moves with the Witton Lane Stand and the Holte End as a backdrop. Edwards had been part of the team that had won the Football League Cup (North), a temporary, wartime substitute for the FA Cup, against Blackpool in May 1944. A 4-2 second-leg win at Villa Park sealed victory for Villa, in front of a 55,000 crowd, after they had lost the first leg 2-1. Edwards scored one of Villa's four second-leg goals but later admitted he had punched the ball into the net. "I was facing an open goal," he said, "when I was pulled down from behind. As I fell, the ball bounced up, so I gave it a mighty right-hander. It went in like a rocket and you could have heard a pin drop when the ref gave a goal. Everyone else knew I had handled it."

# Leading from the Front

RIGHT: Jimmy Hogan, who became manager of Aston Villa in 1936, following the club's first relegation, was an evangelical figure who would hold stage shows to demonstrate the finer points of football coaching and technique. Fred Rinder, the dynamic club chairman, had travelled to Germany to recruit Hogan, then 53, who had been in demand as a coach throughout the continent, notably laying the groundwork for the great Austrian and Hungarian national teams of that era. Rinder's audacious recruitment of Hogan worked: the club were promoted in 1938 and enormous crowds flocked to Villa Park to see a team playing exciting, progressive football under a unique manager.

OPPOSITE: Alex Massie enjoyed a seamless transition from playing to management when, in September 1945, he concluded a decade of stylish service to Villa, as a midfield player, on a Saturday afternoon and had his feet under the manager's desk at the club on the Monday morning. The club had been without a manager since Jimmy Hogan's departure in 1939 to work for the armed forces, at the beginning of the Second World War, and Massie was as smoothly reassuring a presence in the manager's collar and tie as he had been for his previous decade in a Villa jersey, keeping the club in the top half of the First Division table during the immediate postwar years. Behind the scenes, Massie was unhappy at directorial interference throughout his tenure as manager, and in July 1949, having finally had enough, he resigned.

# A Special Backdrop

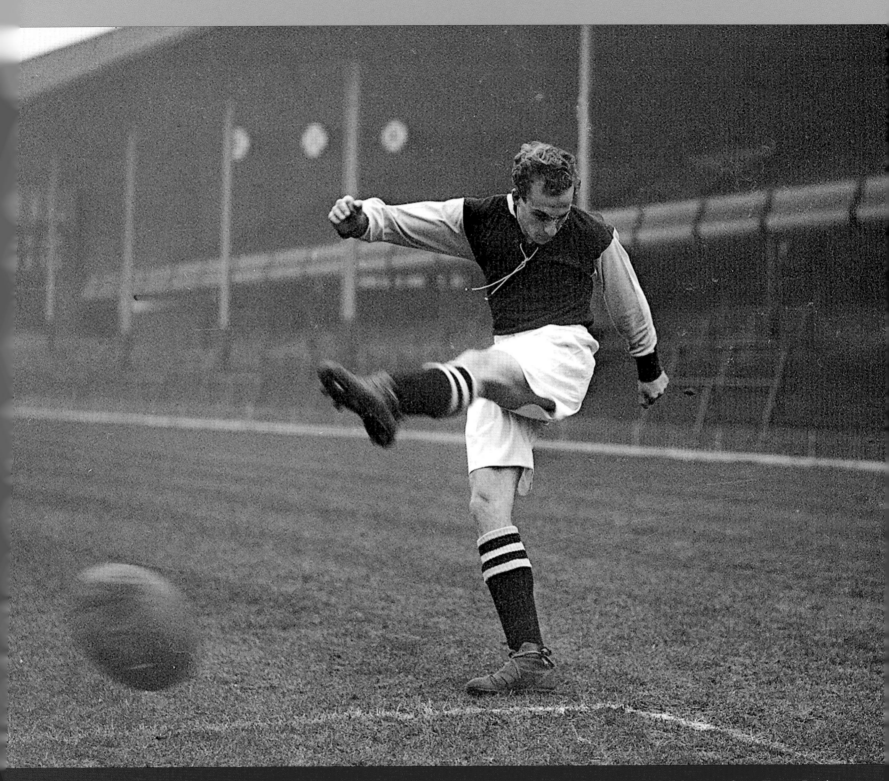

Eddie Lowe demonstrates the effectiveness of his left-footed shooting action from the corner of the penalty box in front of the magnificent Trinity Road Stand at Villa Park. An energetic, determined, midfield player, Lowe joined Villa in 1945 and helped bolster the team during the first half-decade of postwar football. The beautifully ornate, Archibald Leitch-designed, Trinity Road Stand, which was opened in 1922, had 6,500 tip-up seats and an enclosure in front that held 11,000 spectators. Fred Rinder, the visionary Villa chairman, was the inspiration behind the stand, and had spent 33 years overseeing the development of Villa Park into what he described as "the best ground in the kingdom".

# A Standing Arrangement

LEFT: A slightly apprehensive-looking collection of Aston Villa supporters watch as Villa take on Bolton Wanderers in the FA Cup at Villa Park in January 1949. They had good reason to be concerned. This was the second replay of the tie and the third time the clubs had met in nine days. George Edwards and Herbie Smith assuaged any doubts over Villa's progress with the home side's goals in a 2-1 win. The match was played on a Monday and, during those pre-floodlit days, that meant an afternoon kick-off. Even so, almost 50,000 turned up at Villa Park; such was the allure of the Cup that the total attendance for the three matches reached 150,000. Note the predominance of collar and tie and the scarcity of club colours on the terraces. The game was the thing.

A Cup Crescendo
# 1950-1957

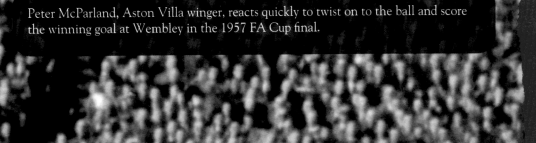

Peter McParland, Aston Villa winger, reacts quickly to twist on to the ball and score the winning goal at Wembley in the 1957 FA Cup final.

> *There have been cleverer sides at Villa Park but none has been in better condition or played better as a team than the present one.*
>
> Eric Houghton, Aston Villa manager, 1957

**1950** George Martin, appointed manager in mid-season, saves Villa from a seemingly certain second relegation and the club concludes the season 15th in the First Division. **1951** Con Martin, an Ireland international centre-half, is converted, early in the 1951/2 season, from being a defender into Villa's first-team goalkeeper by George Martin. **1952** Peter McParland joins Villa from Dundalk. The match with Cardiff City, scheduled for 6th December, is the first to be postponed at Villa Park since the 1930s. **1953** On the eve of a new season, George Martin is dismissed as Villa manager and replaced by Eric Houghton, a Villa goalscoring great of the 1930s. **1954** Government officials finally provide permission for a section of the Witton Lane Stand to be repaired, it having remained badly damaged since being struck by a wartime bomb. **1955** An FA Cup tie with Doncaster Rovers goes to a fourth replay only for Villa to lose 3-1 at the neutral venue of the Hawthorns. **1956** A 3-0 win over West Bromwich Albion at Villa Park on the final day of the season enables Villa to avoid relegation from the First Division. **1957** Villa defeat Manchester United 2-1 at Wembley to win their first FA Cup since 1920. Gerry Hitchens is signed from Cardiff City shortly before Christmas.

Aston Villa players enjoy a day on the golf course at Letchworth, Hertfordshire, in 1953.

Derek Pace, Aston Villa centre-forward, gets to the ball before his team-mate Johnny Dixon to direct a header towards the Manchester United goal at Old Trafford in February 1956. United were chasing the championship and Villa seeking to avoid relegation. A series of eight goals from Pace in 11 games during the run-in at the end of the season proved to be crucial in scooping Villa clear of the Second Division.

Aston Villa goalkeeper Nigel Sims gets to the ball ahead of Duncan Edwards, Manchester United centre-forward, during an encounter at Old Trafford in March 1957. The game would end in a 1-1 draw but the two clubs would meet again at the end of the season in a dramatic FA Cup final.

RIGHT: Villa were widely regarded as certainties to lose the 1957 FA Cup final, in which they would face a Manchester United side that had just won its second successive League Championship title, by an eight-point margin, and that had contested a European Cup semi-final with Real Madrid only nine days previously. Villa, in contrast, had finished the season firmly in mid-table and had needed a fair degree of luck to overcome supposedly better sides en route to the final. Here Frank McGhee, the *Daily Mirror*'s football correspondent, follows the general trend in predicting a Villa capitulation, but the day before the final Billy Walker, the Villa great who was by then Nottingham Forest manager, had predicted a 2-1 triumph for his former club.

# UP FOR THE CUP!

Aston Villa — ALDIS  SAWARD  DIXON (Captn.)  McPARLAND  BERRY  WHELAN  COLMAN  FOULKES  Manchester United

SIMS  DUGDALE  MYERSCOUGH  TAYLOR  BLANCH-FLOWER  WOOD (Captn.)

SELLON  LYNN  CROWTHER  SEWELL  SMITH  PEGG  CHARLTON  EDWARDS  BYRNE (Captn.)

● SALLON'S impression of the twenty-two players who will be fighting out this afternoon's Cup Final at Wembley.

## THE ROAD TO WEMBLEY

ASTON Villa scored 15 goals against 8 on the way to Wembley. Results:

**THIRD ROUND:** Beat Luton 2—0 at home after 2—2 draw.
**FOURTH ROUND:** Beat Middlesbrough 3—2 away.
**FIFTH ROUND:** Beat Bristol City 2—1 at home.
**SIXTH ROUND:** Beat Burnley 2—0 at home after 1—1 draw away.
**SEMI-FINAL:** Beat West Bromwich Albion 1—0 at St. Andrews, Birmingham, after 2—2 draw at Wolverhampton.

MANCHESTER United scored 14 goals against 4. Results:

**THIRD ROUND:** Beat Hartlepools 4—3 away.
**FOURTH ROUND:** Beat Wrexham 5—0 away.
**FIFTH ROUND:** Beat Everton 1—0 at home.
**SIXTH ROUND:** Beat Bournemouth 2—1 away.
**SEMI-FINAL:** Beat Birmingham 2—0 at Hillsborough, Sheffield.

# Goodbye to Villa...half-an-hour after the kick-off

## FRANK McGHEE says: Cup Final will be as good as over by 3.30

SUDDEN death at Wembley. That is what I expect to see on the famous lush green battleground this afternoon—WITH ASTON VILLA AS THE VICTIMS.

I expect to see them killed stone cold dead by a couple of quick stabbing goals in the first half-hour. By 3.30 this afternoon Manchester United should be well on the way to victory.

A win this afternoon will place them alone on a proud pinnacle of glory, above every other team in British Soccer history.

And everything is on their side — TALENT, TEMPERAMENT, TEAM SPIRIT.

### MAN BY MAN

Compare the two teams man by man and Manchester United look a class ahead of Villa in at least nine of the eleven positions.

Villa goalkeeper Nigel Sims is as good, maybe even better, than United's Ray Wood on current form. And outside left Peter McParland, the flying Irishman, has perhaps slightly more match-winning star quality than David Pegg.

In every other position, the Villa man must give best to his Manchester United counter-part.

Another vital match-winning factor on United's side is the occasion itself.

The arrogant young men of Manchester are used to the big matches. The size of the crowd, the desperate importance of it all won't cause any dry mouths, stomach cramps and trembling knees in THEIR camp.

Four of them, 'keeper them apart from any other team in the country.

By 3.30 this afternoon Manchester United should be well on the way to victory.

I take United to make this D for Double day—the double of Cup and League which hasn't been done this century.

The double I never expected to see the double which even Manchester United didn't think possible and which is now just ninety minutes away.

Their achievements already this season in the League, the European Cup and the F.A. Cup have set them apart from any other team in the country.

A win this afternoon will place them alone on a proud pinnacle of glory, above every other team in British Soccer history.

Villa goalkeeper Nigel Sims is as good, maybe even better, than United's Ray Wood on current form.

### FRIGHTENING

To Villa it will all be bewilderingly new, strange, frightening.

That's why it's my guess that they will fail in the first half hour.

And even if they manage to hang on that long, the best I can see them achieving is a draw and a Goodison Park replay on Thursday.

Villa fans are pinning much of their faith in the tremendous resurgence of team spirit, brought about by that solid, sensible Ray Wood, skipper and left back Roger Byrne, the most improved player in the country, left half mighty Duncan Edwards and Tommy Taylor, the best centre forward in England, know it all.

They will walk out with the easy familiarity of men who know the dressing rooms, the long walk from the tunnel and the billiard-table turf intimately from international experience.

The others have all lived through the fiery baptism of European Cup matches where the noise and the strain make Wembley Stadium seem like a whispering gallery at midnight.

### AN OMEN

Soccer citizen, manager Eric Houghton.

He has made them proud of their great club again—and they are entitled to feel proud on this season's showing.

But even in team spirit, Manchester United can match them. Look at what happened before they travelled down to London yesterday.

Inside left Dennis Viollet met Manchester United manager Matt Busby at breakfast knowing that he had a great chance of a place in the Cup Final.

He could have kept quiet about the slight nagging pain from an old groin injury. Instead he spoke up: "If I played I might let the side down. We can't take that risk."

Notice the "We." That, my friends, is team spirit.

So in goes Bobby Charlton, the nineteen-year-old who was born to play football, nephew of one of the most famous Cup fighters of all time—Newcastle United's Jackie Milburn.

THAT TOO COULD BE AN OMEN?

## ASTON VILLA
### Light blue, narrow claret stripes

SIMS
2 LYNN        3 ALDIS
4 CROWTHER   5 DUGDALE   6 SAWARD
7 SMITH  8 SEWELL  MYERSCOUGH 10 DIXON 11 McPARLAND

Kick-off: 3 p.m.    Referee: F. Coultas (Hull)

11 PEGG  10 CHARLTON  9 TAYLOR  8 WHELAN  7 BERRY
6 EDWARDS  5 BLANCHFLOWER  4 COLMAN
3 BYRNE        2 FOULKES
WOOD

### White, red edgings

## MANCHESTER U.

### B.B.C. TELEVISION
2.15—" How they got there " film.
2.30—Community singing.
2.55—Presentation of teams to the Duke of Edinburgh.
3.0—Kick-off.
3.45—Half-time.  3.55—Second half.
4.45—Presentation of Cup and medals by the Queen and the Duke of Edinburgh.
### RADIO—LIGHT PROGRAMME
2.30-5.0—Commentaries with summaries at half- and full-time.

## Just right, says Houghton

ASTON VILLA travelled by coach to London yesterday and then went on to Wembley.

They paraded round practically every inch of the turf, and were delighted to find that they have been allocated the North dressing room.

"That is the 'lucky' dressing room out of which most of the Wembley winners have come.

"We're all fit. The players couldn't be in happier trim and after our long and careful inspection we feel that this pitch is made for us," Eric Houghton said last night.

### RESULTS
THIRD DIVISION SOUTH.—Bournemouth 1 (Brown, Norris, Shipwright p.k., Longmuir), Watford 2 (Longmuir), Watford 1, 1—2.
REPRESENTATIVE MATCH.—England 1, Young England 2 (at Highbury).

# BIG CONFESSION SLAMMED

ON the eve of the Cup Final the Football League condemned the Players' Union "Big Confession" by players who have taken under the counter payments.

After a meeting lasting most of yesterday the League said:

"We will not negotiate with the Union or anyone else under threats or in impossible conditions."

The Union have been busy all this week collecting signatures of members who have received illegal payments.

The Union hope that these confessions will persuade the League and F.A. to declare a general amnesty and change the regulations which forbid players to accept more than a £10 signing on fee.

But the Union insist that they will only co-operate in this bid to clean up Soccer if:

1.—No action is taken against players who give evidence.

2.—The current suspensions are lifted on Ray Daniel, Willie Fraser, Billy Elliott, Johnny Hannigan and Ken Chisholm.

The League in yesterday's statement said:

THEY were willing to negotiate with the Union but not under threats.

THEY were willing to accept any evidence of illegal payments, but it "must be given unconditionally."

THEY regretted that a registered player of the League had made threatening statements in the Press after holding a responsible position with the Union for so short a period.

THEY thought that such action could only bring the game into disrepute and could not benefit the majority of League players.

## CROSSWORD

### ACROSS
1, Whiten; 6, Fastener; 9, Frees; 10, Poet; 11, Inventor; 13, Scientist; 15, Child; 14, Vague; 17, Unctuous; 19, Foster; 21, Girl; 24, Invoice; 25, Arab; 27, Away; 29, Aslant; 31, Sing; 30, Reply; 32, Port; 33, Border; 34, Breaches; 35, Rubber.

### DOWN
1, Foreigner; 2, Resort; 3, Our boss; 4, Idiot; 5, Sweetness; 6, Generous; 7, River; 8, Gay; 12, Make eyes; 14, Lounge; 16, Rebukes; 17, 20, State; 21, Fit; 22, Candies; 23, Character; 24, Swiss town; 26, Deer; 26, Harvest; 28, Press; 31, Beverage.

### Yesterday's Solution
DEPOT PASTE
E ABIGAIL V
APRON WROTE
TREE C MOON
HOD PARAPET
N MORON O
R REFUTED FAR
ERAS PAPA
ABUSE WORST
C SERVILE T
TITTLE TODDY

# A Crucial Collision

LEFT: Peter McParland, Aston Villa outside-left, and Ray Wood, Manchester United goalkeeper, in the immediate aftermath of their sixth-minute collision in the 1957 FA Cup final. McParland had shoulder-charged the goalkeeper, a legitimate and accepted aspect of the game of football in the 1950s. Kenneth Wolstenholme, the BBC's commentator at the Cup final, described it immediately as a "fair charge". The Villa man would eventually get back to his feet and continue playing, but Wood was carried off on a stretcher, having sustained a fractured cheekbone – although, with no substitutes allowed in British football at the time, he would later return to the field to play, gingerly, and surprisingly well, on the wing.

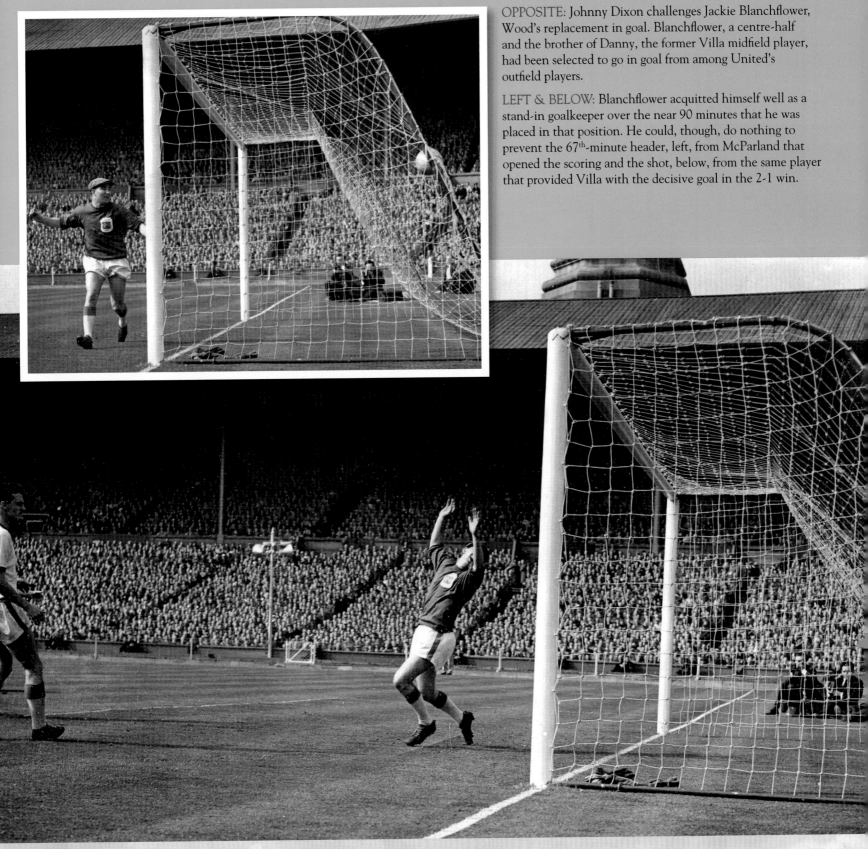

OPPOSITE: Johnny Dixon challenges Jackie Blanchflower, Wood's replacement in goal. Blanchflower, a centre-half and the brother of Danny, the former Villa midfield player, had been selected to go in goal from among United's outfield players.

LEFT & BELOW: Blanchflower acquitted himself well as a stand-in goalkeeper over the near 90 minutes that he was placed in that position. He could, though, do nothing to prevent the 67th-minute header, left, from McParland that opened the scoring and the shot, below, from the same player that provided Villa with the decisive goal in the 2-1 win.

# Wembley Wonders

RIGHT: Villa players and the team mascot relax and
enjoy themselves on the Wembley pitch after the 1957
FA Cup final. The Villa players are, from left to right:
Jackie Sewell, Jimmy Dugdale, Stan Lynn, Peter Aldis
and Johnny Dixon.

45

# Cup Cheer

RIGHT: A suitably delighted section of Aston Villa supporters wait outside the Council House in Birmingham for the team to return to the city and show off the FA Cup.

# –LEGENDS– Johnny Dixon

It seems appropriate that Johnny Dixon should have arrived at Aston Villa through a romantic gesture. As a boy in Hebburn-on-Tyne, he had been so taken by the Birmingham club's name that he had written to Villa Park asking for a trial. His first full season establishing himself in the Villa first team, 1946/7, marked the resumption of the FA Cup and First Division after seven years' absence owing to the Second World War. A speedy inside-forward with an infectious grin and enormous enthusiasm for the game, Dixon symbolized the new, fresh face of Villa after the fatiguing war years.

Not only was Dixon the team captain for the 1957 FA Cup final but he scored five crucial goals to help power the team to Wembley and was involved in setting up both of Peter McParland's goals in the final. He would later admit glancing up at the Cup in the Royal Box minutes from the end of the match to find his eyes were filling with tears. He bowed out at 37 years of age with a goal in a 4-1 victory over Sheffield Wednesday, though he felt that the club had released him too soon. After six years working for Villa as a youth coach, Dixon, a teetotaller and non-smoker who played for the Villa All Stars into his early seventies, opened an ironmonger's shop in Sutton Coldfield.

Johnny Dixon climbs above Jack Stelling of Sunderland to head for goal in front of a packed Witton Lane Stand at Villa Park in September 1952. Dixon would score one of his 144 Villa goals in this 3-0 win.

ABOVE: Billy Moore, the Villa trainer, and Johnny Dixon's team-mates chair the genial captain at Wembley after the 2-1 victory over Manchester United in the 1957 Cup final.

> *Pick Johnny Dixon up and get him on your shoulders after the game with the Cup and we'll all gather round for the photograph.*
>
> Billy Moore, the confident Aston Villa trainer, prior to the 1957 FA Cup final

Stan Lynn, the Aston Villa right-back, seeks to usher the ball away from the attentions of Bobby Charlton, the Manchester United winger, during a meeting of the 1957 FA Cup finalists in October of that year. Nigel Sims, the Villa goalkeeper, prepares for all eventualities.

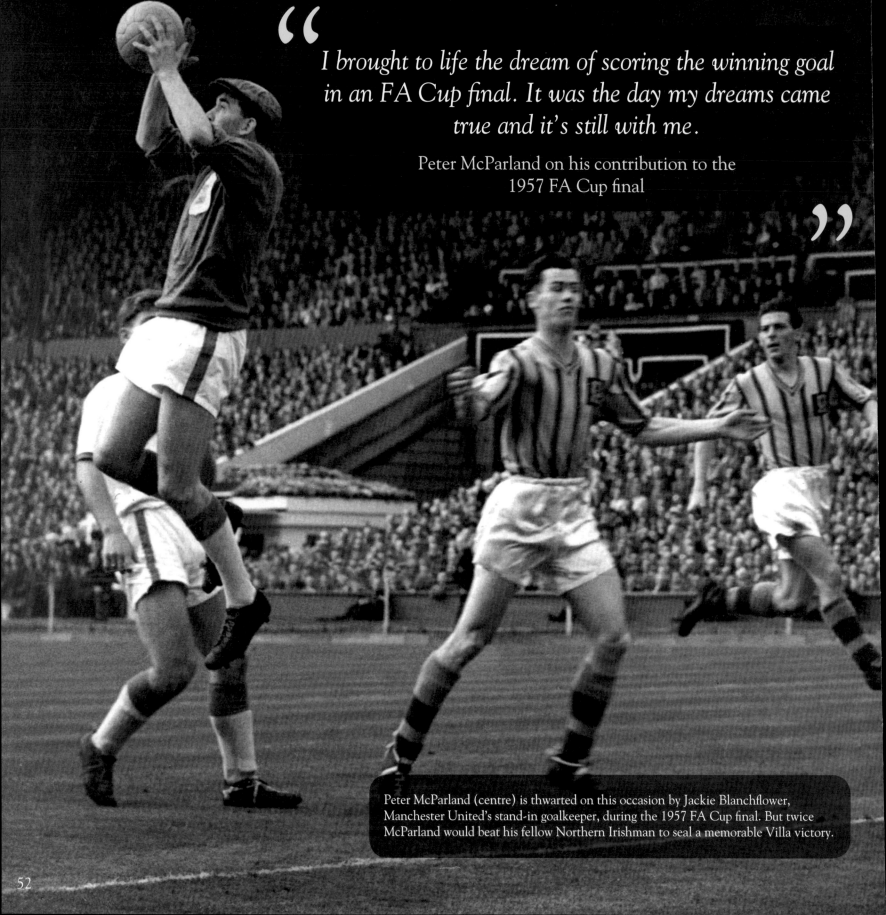

> "I brought to life the dream of scoring the winning goal in an FA Cup final. It was the day my dreams came true and it's still with me."

Peter McParland on his contribution to the 1957 FA Cup final

Peter McParland (centre) is thwarted on this occasion by Jackie Blanchflower, Manchester United's stand-in goalkeeper, during the 1957 FA Cup final. But twice McParland would beat his fellow Northern Irishman to seal a memorable Villa victory.

## FOOTBALL STATS

### Peter McParland

Name: Peter James McParland

Born: 1934

Playing Career: 1950-1971

Clubs: Dundalk, Aston Villa, Wolverhampton Wanderers, Plymouth Argyle, Worcester City, Atlanta Chiefs, Glentoran

Aston Villa Appearances: 341

Aston Villa Goals: 121

Northern Ireland Appearances: 34

Goals: 10

BELOW: Peter McParland (extreme right) awaits his turn to be introduced to Prince Philip, the Duke of Edinburgh, as the Aston Villa players go through the formalities before kick-off in the 1957 FA Cup final; this was to be the most dramatic club match of McParland's life.

# –LEGENDS–

## Peter McParland

It is for the 1957 FA Cup final that Peter McParland is immortalized in the minds of Villa followers even if it was one of his most subdued appearances for the club. For much of the hour of play following his sixth-minute collision with Ray Wood, which led to the Manchester United goalkeeper's removal from the action, McParland had a quiet game. Not only had he been badly shaken by the incident itself but he had subsequently received a jarring elbow in the face from Bill Foulkes, the Manchester United right-back, and had had his every touch jeered by the United fans. Yet his two, sharp goals in four minutes late in the second half transformed a potentially painful afternoon into a triumphant one, and won Villa their only FA Cup in nine decades.

Far from that FA Cup final being the peak of this goalscoring winger's career, McParland, only 23 at the time of that match, developed into an even finer player, even though, at six feet one inches, he was unusually tall for a wide player. He scored five of Northern Ireland's six goals at the 1958 World Cup finals as they coursed through to the quarter-finals, and when, after nine years at Villa, McParland started a match for the first time as centre-forward, in the 1961 League Cup final second leg, with Rotherham United, he struck the goal that won the Cup. Surprisingly, Villa allowed him, still only 27 years old, to be transferred to Wolverhampton Wanderers for a £25,000 fee just four months after that triumph.

# Ups and Downs
## 1958-1969

Aston Villa goalkeeper Nigel Sims clutches the ball safely during the first leg of the 1961 League Cup final away to Rotherham United at the Yorkshire club's homely Millmoor ground. This was the first final of the new competition and Villa would win it to begin a long love affair with the League Cup.

"
*The potential of this club is enormous.*

Joe Mercer on becoming Aston Villa manager in 1958

**1958** Floodlights are installed at Villa Park. Eric Houghton resigns as manager in November and is replaced a month later by Joe Mercer. **1959** Villa lose out in the FA Cup semi-finals to Nottingham Forest, managed by Billy Walker, and are relegated for the second time in their history.

**1960** Promotion back to the First Division is secured at the first attempt and Villa again reach the FA Cup semi-finals, only to be beaten by Wolverhampton Wanderers.

**1961** Gerry Hitchens, a prolific goalscorer, is transferred to Internazionale of Milan for £85,000. A 3-2 aggregate victory over Rotherham United in the two-legged League Cup final sees Villa win the tournament at the first time of asking. **1963** Villa reach a second League Cup final but this time are defeated by Birmingham City 3-1 on aggregate.

**1964** Joe Mercer resigns as manager on grounds of ill-health, to be replaced by Dick Taylor. **1967** When Villa collect only two points from their final eight fixtures, relegation to the Second Division becomes inevitable and Dick Taylor is dismissed and replaced by Tommy Cummings. **1968** Mike Ferguson, a winger, becomes Villa's new record signing when he arrives from Blackburn Rovers for a £50,000 fee. With Villa in bottom place in the Second Division, fans agitate for the Board of Directors to resign. The following month the Board are duly bought out by a consortium of new directors spearheaded by chairman Doug Ellis. Tommy Docherty replaces Tommy Cummings as Aston Villa manager.

**1969** A successful share issue in Villa allows Docherty to spend £400,000 on players and Villa become the most expensively assembled side in the Second Division.

Young Villa players participate in a practice match with their senior colleagues during the pre-season of 1958. With Villa having won the FA Cup the previous year and with several budding youngsters at the club, the future looked bright; the following decade, however, would prove to be the most testing of any in the club's history.

Ray Wood, left, Manchester United goalkeeper, shows there are no hard feelings as
he chats happily with Peter McParland, the Aston Villa forward, with whom he had
collided so dramatically in the 1957 FA Cup final. The two are reunited here before a
league fixture at Villa Park in March 1958.

John Sharples, a young left-back looking to break into the Villa first team in the 1958/9 season, passes time in the summer of 1958 by mowing the lawn, while Valerie Walker, his 16-year-old girlfriend, gets the shears out to do some edging. Even in the more formal Fifties, both look perhaps that little bit too smartly dressed for their dual tasks. Sharples would get a run in the Villa team early in the 1958/9 season, but his career with Villa would go no further than that.

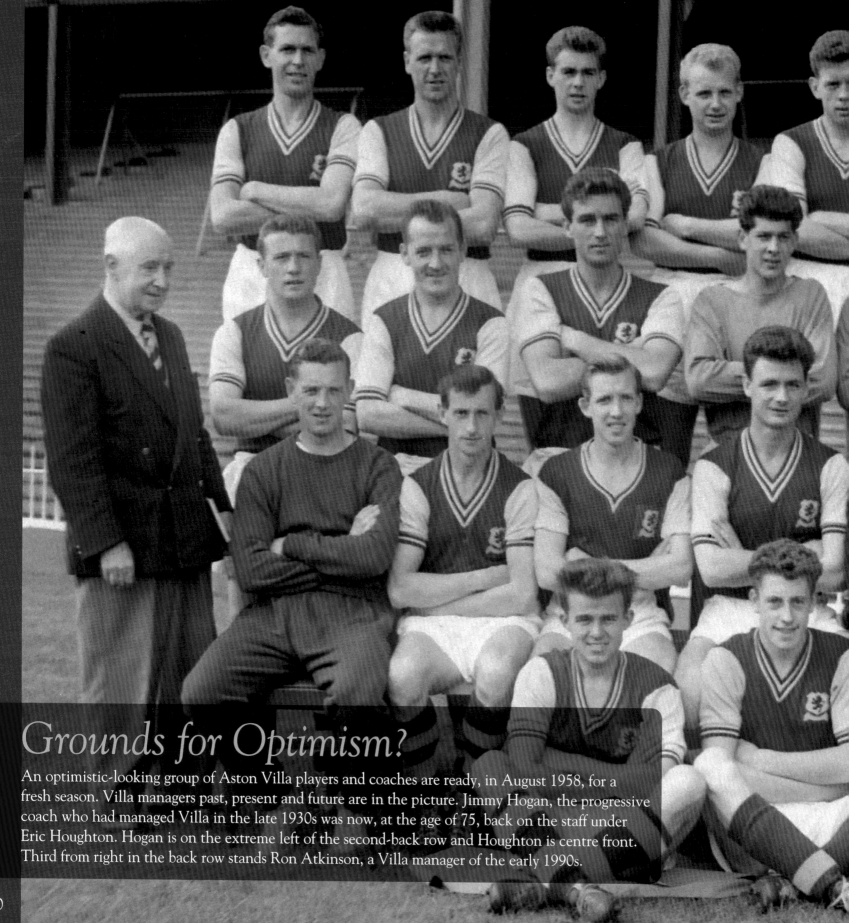

# Grounds for Optimism?

An optimistic-looking group of Aston Villa players and coaches are ready, in August 1958, for a fresh season. Villa managers past, present and future are in the picture. Jimmy Hogan, the progressive coach who had managed Villa in the late 1930s was now, at the age of 75, back on the staff under Eric Houghton. Hogan is on the extreme left of the second-back row and Houghton is centre front. Third from right in the back row stands Ron Atkinson, a Villa manager of the early 1990s.

The pre-season optimism here would quickly evaporate as Villa suffered a catastrophic series of results in the remaining months of 1958. Houghton would resign in late November and five months after that the club would plummet into the Second Division.

61

# A Link with the Past

Gerry Hitchens, the Villa centre-forward, prepares to take advantage of any slip that might occur as Manchester United goalkeeper Harry Gregg and Bill Foulkes, his right-back, combine to try to close down an Aston Villa attack. The barrelled roof of the Witton Lane Stand forms an interesting backdrop to the action. It dated back to 1897 and the original construction of Villa Park and had housed the dressing rooms prior to the opening of the Trinity Road Stand in the 1920s. The Witton Lane Stand roof would survive until 1963, when it was demolished to be replaced by a rather more functional, level covering.

LEFT: In this meeting with United in the autumn of 1960, Villa, newly promoted to the First Division, enjoyed a 3-1 victory. They went on to conclude the season in the top half of the First Division table.

# –LEGENDS–

## Gerry Hitchens

As a streamlined striker, Gerry Hitchens was the perfect man to spearhead Aston Villa's transition from the 1950s and the era of baggy shorts to the faster and sleeker football of the 1960s. Hitchens would be a huge success for Villa, quickly clicking and scoring 11 goals in the second half of the 1957/8 season. He would go on to be Villa's leading goalscorer in each of his subsequent three full seasons with the club, albeit jointly with Peter McParland in 1959/60, when their dual goalscoring immediately retrieved Villa from the ignominy of the Second Division.

   Nicknamed "Champion the Wonder Horse" by team-mates because of his speed across the ground, his pace, allied to quick reactions, made him a forceful attacker. When Hitchens hit 42 goals in the 1960/1 season, his record attracted the interest of Internazionale of Milan, and although Villa directors insisted he would not be sold, Hitchens was soon whisked off to Italy, where he spent the remainder of the decade, successfully plying his trade with various clubs.

> *He was a flier. If he got the ball on the run then that was it – the defenders were gone.*
>
> Peter McParland on Gerry Hitchens

## FOOTBALL
## –STATS–

### Gerry Hitchens

Name: Gerald Archibald Hitchens

Born: 1934

Died: 1983

Playing Career: 1953-1971

Clubs: Kidderminster Harriers, Cardiff City, Aston Villa, Internazionale, Torino, Atalanta, Cagliari, Worcester City, Merthyr Tydfil

Aston Villa Appearances: 160

Aston Villa Goals: 96

England Appearances: 7

Goals: 5

Gerry (far left) in Glasgow with fellow Britons John Charles (second left), Denis Law (second right) and Joe Baker prior to representing the Italian League against the Scottish League at Hampden Park in November 1961. All four were playing for major clubs in Italy at the time.

ABOVE: Eric Houghton, left, Aston Villa manager, watches as Gerry Hitchens, alongside Meriel, his wife, signs for Villa from Cardiff City shortly before Christmas 1957.

LEFT: Gerry window-shopping with Jimmy Greaves, another great English goalscorer of the 1960s, at London Airport, prior to the departure of the England squad for the 1962 World Cup finals in Chile, where Gerry would score England's goal in the 3-1 defeat to Brazil in the quarter-finals.

# The **1961** League Cup Final

> *At first we didn't want the League Cup but later in the season its matches replaced the drudgery of training, then we got a run going – and wee bonuses – so the players started to become quite happy with the new Cup.*
>
> Peter McParland

LEFT: Aston Villa goalkeeper Nigel Sims bravely dives at the feet of Keith Bambridge of Rotherham United during the first leg of the 1961 League Cup final at the Yorkshire club's Millmoor home, where slightly more than 12,000 crammed in to see the first instalment of the first final of the new competition. Rotherham scored twice shortly after half-time to win 2-0 in a match that also saw a penalty from Villa's Stan Lynn saved by Roy Ironside, the Rotherham goalkeeper. Villa played poorly in the first leg but made up for it in the return at Villa Park. Goals from Alan O'Neill and Harry Burrows levelled the aggregate, and Peter McParland scored the winning goal in extra-time to make Villa the first winners of the League Cup.

67

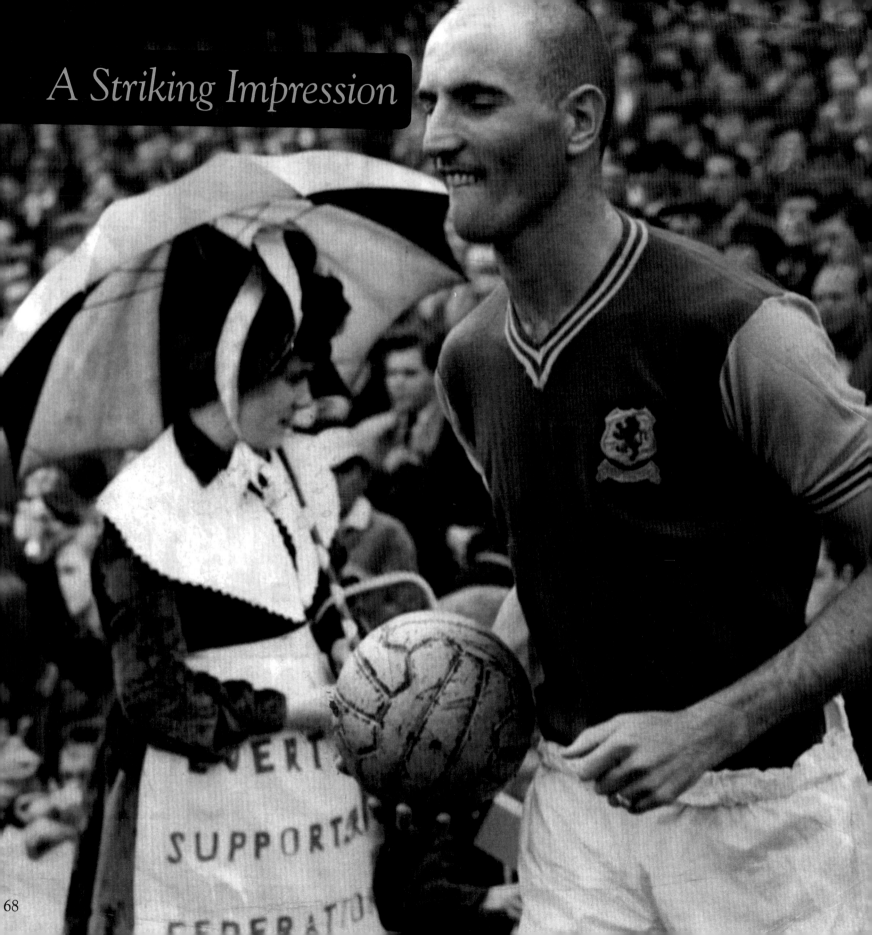

ABOVE: Birmingham City goalkeeper Johnny Schofield gets down to save under an exuberant challenge from Bobby Thomson during the second leg of the 1963 League Cup final at Villa Park. The Witton Lane Stand, undergoing reconstruction, is in the background.

LEFT: Derek Dougan trots out for his Aston Villa debut at Everton's Goodison Park in August 1961 sporting a pawky grin and a newly shaven head, both of which signalled his individualistic nature. Signed from Blackburn Rovers, Dougan, a centre-forward, would score three goals in his first four Villa appearances, but in September 1961, hours after Villa's victory over Rotherham United in the first League Cup final, Dougan was a passenger in a Vauxhall Velox driven by Bobby Thomson that crashed into a tree, instantly killing Malcolm Williams, a 23-year-old reporter from the *Wolverhampton Express & Star* who had also been a passenger. Thomson, many years later, stated that Dougan, in a state of extreme drunkenness, had distracted Thomson, making him lose control of the car and crash.

Dougan's injuries in the crash saw him miss the subsequent three months of the season and he would never quite spark consistently again for Villa before being transferred to Peterborough United in 1963.

Villa centre-forward Bobby Thomson in the first leg of the 1963 League Cup final spectacularly challenges Stan Lynn, Birmingham City full-back, who had moved to St Andrews from Villa in 1961. Thomson would, later in 1963, join him in exile.

"King of the Road"
AUSTIN HEALEY
AUSTIN GIPSY
Swim and keep fit
- at your Local

Bobby Thomson watches Johnny Schofield collect the ball during the League Cup final in May 1963. Thomson, one of Villa's most prolific goalscorers during the early 1960s, scored the Villa goal in their first-leg 3-1 defeat in late May 1963. With the second leg, four days later, ending 0-0, the Cup went to St Andrews.

# Up Close and Personal

RIGHT: Denis Law, Manchester United forward, is given the benefit of some Aston Villa supporters' full and frank advice as he is led to the dressing room following his dismissal in Villa's 4-0 victory over his team in November 1963. Police had intervened to usher Law off the field after he had been sent off by Jim Carr, the referee, for kicking Alan Deakin while the Villa player lay on the ground. Villa were fighting relegation and United chasing the title, so the thrashing doled out to his team was a bitter one for Law to undergo.

# That Sinking Feeling

ABOVE: Mick Wright, the Aston Villa full-back, sets off in pursuit of Bobby Tambling, the Chelsea winger, during a league encounter between the sides early on in the 1966/7 season. The Holte End, in the background, would still be busy during that season but matches such as this one, which saw Villa 4-0 down at half-time and on the end of a 6-2 full-time defeat, prepared all associated with the club for the drop.

RIGHT: Alan Deakin takes to the field for an FA Cup tie with Liverpool at Anfield in February 1967. A local Birmingham lad and one of Mercer's Minors, a group of talented young players who had come through the club's youth system in the late 1950s, Deakin had established himself as a Villa regular during the 1960/1 season, the club's first in the top flight after winning the Second Division in 1960. With Villa relegation-bound in 1967, there was, unfortunately, no succour to be found in the FA Cup that year, this tie with Liverpool concluding in a 1-0 defeat.

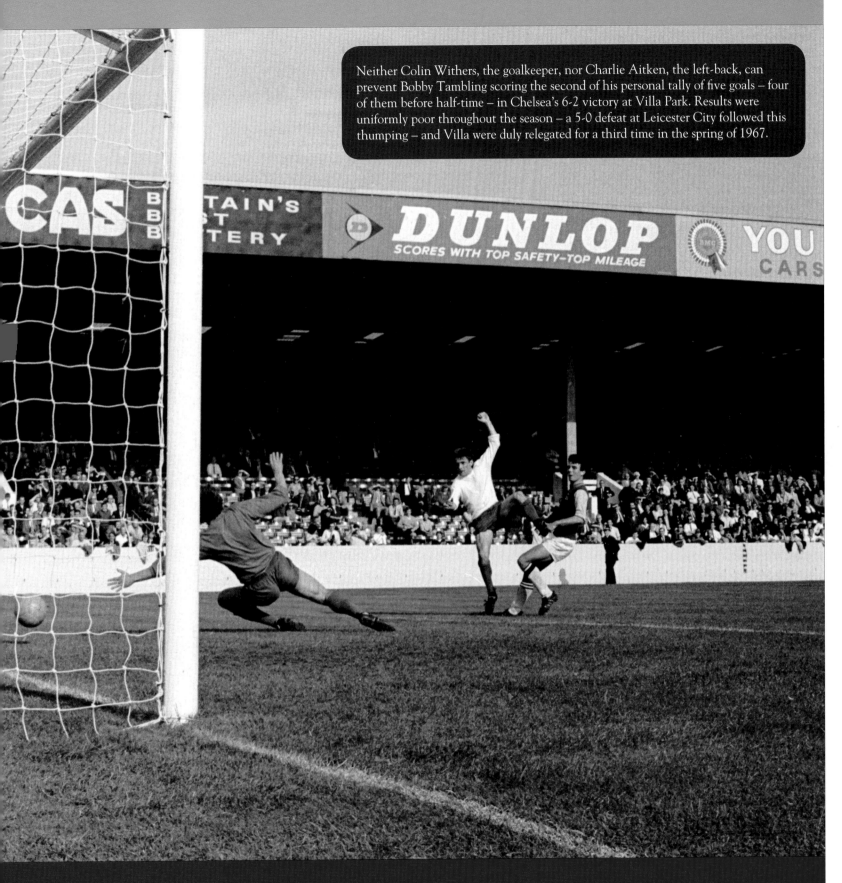

Neither Colin Withers, the goalkeeper, nor Charlie Aitken, the left-back, can prevent Bobby Tambling scoring the second of his personal tally of five goals – four of them before half-time – in Chelsea's 6-2 victory at Villa Park. Results were uniformly poor throughout the season – a 5-0 defeat at Leicester City followed this thumping – and Villa were duly relegated for a third time in the spring of 1967.

# Fun and Games

Tommy Docherty looks the part of the go-ahead young manager of the late 1960s as he relaxes at home by playing Subbuteo with his children. Appointed Aston Villa manager in November 1968, he brought a degree of energy and liveliness to the club, along with sharp one-liners and possibly even gimmickry. He made Jimmy Brown, at 15, the youngest first-team player in Villa's history, had a carpet of astro-turf laid in his office and endeared himself to the Holte End by walking the length of the pitch pre-match before bowing in front of them. Brought in as manager by a new Board of Directors, Docherty's enthusiasm saved Villa from a second successive relegation in 1969, but when he left in January 1970, having spent liberally on players, Villa were hurtling towards the Third Division.

Any player who crossed Tommy Docherty could quickly find himself out in the cold. Barrie Hole, the Villa midfield player and a Wales international, on arrival at Blackburn railway station in December 1969 to discuss a return to Rovers, his former club, from whom he had been signed by Villa for a club record fee of £65,000 in the September of the previous year. Hole had gone on strike at Villa after being fined by Tommy Docherty but his return to Blackburn Rovers did not go through and he would be restored to the Villa team after Docherty was dismissed as manager in January 1970.

BLACKBURN

# Vintage Villa
## 1970-1979

> " We all know about Villa's vast potential but now we are on the verge of doing something about it. This club is near to an explosion.
>
> Ron Saunders, Aston Villa manager, 1975 "

Aston Villa captain Ian Ross shows off the League Cup to Villa fans in Birmingham from the balcony of the Council House after the Wembley victory over Norwich City in 1975.

**1970** With Aston Villa bottom of the Second Division, Tommy Docherty is sacked in January and replaced by Vic Crowe – but the new manager is unable to prevent relegation to the Third Division. **1971** Despite being the better side throughout, Villa lose the League Cup final 2-0 to Tottenham Hotspur. **1972** Villa win the Third Division with a divisional record total of 70 points and an average home crowd of just under 32,000. **1973** Charlie Aitken sets a new appearance record for Villa when he wears the claret and blue for the 479th time on 22nd December. **1974** Vic Crowe is dismissed and replaced as manager by Ron Saunders on 4th June. **1975** A 1-0 victory over Norwich City at Wembley gives Villa the League Cup and Saunders' side go on to secure promotion back to the First Division. **1977** Villa win the League Cup by defeating Everton 3-2 in a second replay of the final, at Old Trafford. Ken McNaught becomes Villa's new record signing when he is purchased from Everton for a £200,000 fee. The stylish new North Stand is opened, with seating for 4,000 and a standing enclosure for 6,000 fans in front. **1978** Villa go on their longest run in Europe to date, ended only by defeat to Barcelona on a 4-3 aggregate in the UEFA Cup quarter-finals. **1979** Andy Gray is sold to Wolverhampton Wanderers for a British record fee of £1,469,000. Villa's final match of the decade sees teenage striker Gary Shaw hit a hat-trick in a 3-1 win at Bristol City.

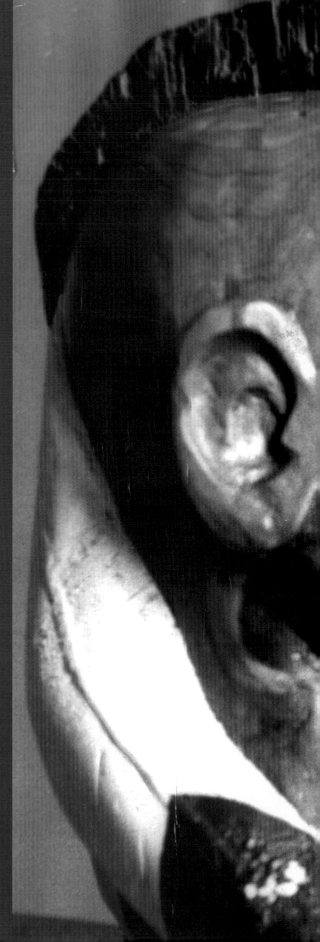

Vic Crowe, who became Aston Villa manager in January 1970, with a Native American carving that had been presented to the club during the 1969 tour of the USA.

# A Touch of Style

Villa did exceptionally well to reach the 1971 League Cup final, given that they were, at the time, a Third Division side. Particularly memorable was the two-legged semi-final, in which they faced Manchester United. The first leg, at Old Trafford, saw Villa draw 1-1 and here striker Andy Lochhead celebrates enthusiastically after putting the ball in the United net.

A crowd of 60,000 rolled up at Villa Park one week later, for the return match, only two days before Christmas Day 1970. Again Lochhead scored the opening goal, and with the score at 1-1 in the second half, and 2-2 on aggregate, Pat McMahon scored Villa's second goal to take the club to Wembley. United's goalkeeper in both legs was Jimmy Rimmer, who would, later in the 1970s, make the switch to Villa.

# The **1971** League Cup Final

Brian Godfrey, the Aston Villa captain, and Alan Mullery, his counterpart at Tottenham Hotspur, witness the toss of the coin by referee Jim Finney before the League Cup final at Wembley in February 1971.

Brian Godfrey, the Aston Villa midfield player, challenges Martin Chivers, the Tottenham striker, during the 1971 League Cup final.

BELOW: Andy Lochhead, the Aston Villa striker, jumps for the ball with Peter Collins, the Tottenham centre-back, as Willie Anderson, the Villa winger, watches and waits.

ABOVE: Bruce Rioch, the Aston Villa midfield player, clears as Alan Gilzean of Tottenham and Charlie Aitken of Villa keep an eye on proceedings. The 1971 League Cup final with Tottenham was a rare and very welcome taste of the big time for a Villa side that was then ploughing along in Third Division football.

Ian "Chico" Hamilton and Phil Beal of Tottenham appear almost to have the pitch to themselves as the 1971 League Cup final rages on.

Villa had most of the game and performed much better than Tottenham, then one of Europe's leading clubs, in the final but, agonizingly, two late goals from Martin Chivers snatched victory from Villa. Here Fred Turnbull (centre-half), tackling Chivers, John Dunn (goalkeeper) and Keith Bradley (right-back) cannot prevent Chivers' shot squeezing into the net.

# Crowd Pleasers

A packed Holte End oversees Andy Lochhead harassing the Bournemouth defence in mid-February 1972. This match, which saw Villa pitted against prominent rivals for promotion from the Third Division, had been anticipated for weeks and produced a record attendance for the division of 48,110. Goals from Geoff Vowden and Andy Lochhead gave Villa a vital 2-1 win and set them up nicely to clinch the Third Division title.

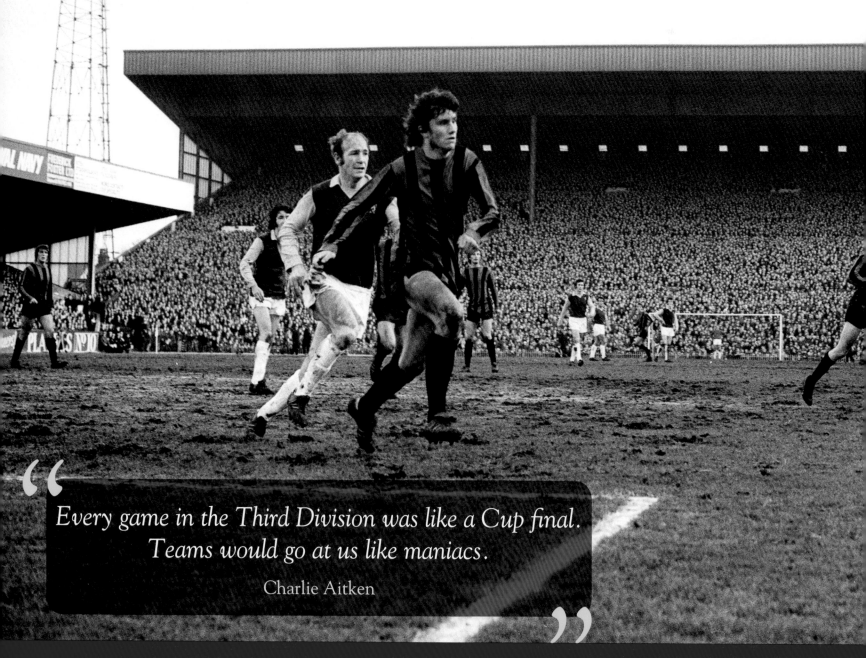

*Every game in the Third Division was like a Cup final. Teams would go at us like maniacs.*

Charlie Aitken

LEFT: Youngsters race back to their places on the Witton End to evade the long arm of the law after celebrating exuberantly a goal in the match with Bournemouth.

BELOW: Jim Cumbes, a goalkeeper signed by Villa from West Bromwich Albion in 1971, combined top-level football with a career in first-class cricket. You could do that in the 1960s and 1970s. Here he makes a point-blank save in the encounter with Bournemouth.

Keith Leonard (centre) and Chris Nicholl (right) in an aerial battle with Stewart Houston, Manchester United full-back, before an entranced mid-1970s Villa Park crowd. Leonard, a striker with a more than useful goals to games ratio and a Birmingham boy who came through the Villa youth ranks to make his debut in spring 1974, was sadly forced to retire from football after suffering a serious knee injury early in the 1975/6 season. Nicholl, a centre-back signed by Vic Crowe in 1972, did much to stabilize the team as Villa climbed slowly back from the Third to the First Division.

BROWNHILLS
5151

# That Seventies Style

Ian Ross, a signing from Liverpool, and Vic Crowe, the Villa manager between 1970 and 1974, show off the latest in early 1970s gear. They may look ready to party but they are actually preparing to get down to pre-season training in the summer of 1972.

Ron Saunders might equally have been preparing to audition for a role in *The Sweeney* as patrolling the Villa Park touchline.

95

# Back on Track

Charlie Aitken, the Aston Villa left-back, and scorer of the second goal in this 2-0 defeat of Manchester United at Villa Park in February 1975, raises his arms as his powerful header from near the edge of the penalty area sails pleasingly into the United net. Aitken then turns away, ready to accept his due congratulations as a large batch of United fans in the 40,000 all-ticket crowd look on in displeasure. Bobby McDonald (far left) and Brian Little watch anxiously as the ball hits the target before they pursue the happy goalscorer. This vital victory, over their chief promotion rivals in the Second Division that season, was essential for Villa's push for promotion, which they clinched two months later, concluding the season in second position, three points behind United.

# -LEGENDS-

## Charlie Aitken

The odds were set against Charlie Aitken making it as an Aston Villa player at all, far less to his going on to become the player with the greatest number of club appearances to his name. A middle-class boy from Edinburgh, his ambition was to attend university, and he devoted as much of his sporting spare time to rugby as he did to football. On arrival at Villa for a trial at 16, Aitken was horrified by the lack of athleticism and fitness among his fellow players and he describes himself as "traumatized" by the bawling and shouting of the training staff. Poorly paid in the third team, he considered returning to Scotland; but once he was given his first-team debut, at 18, in the spring of 1961, he never looked back.

An overlapping full-back with great game-reading powers and a perceptive and engaging individual, Charlie quickly became a mainstay of the team and remained with Villa throughout the trials and tribulations of the 1960s and the first half of the 1970s. A disagreement with Villa manager Ron Saunders soured his departure, but there was compensation in going on from that to enjoy the adventure of playing for the New York Cosmos alongside Pelé in the late 1970s.

> *I just loved being out on the pitch playing football.*
>
> Charlie Aitken

Charlie Aitken, as eager and enthusiastic for the Villa cause as ever, calls for the ball at Villa Park in 1975. Fourteen years after his Villa debut, Aitken remained a fixture in the team, a near-automatic selection for the left-back position.

## FOOTBALL
# –STATS–

### Charlie Aitken

Name: Charles Alexander Aitken

Born: 1942

Playing Career: 1961-1977

Clubs: Aston Villa, New York Cosmos

Aston Villa Appearances: 660

Aston Villa Goals: 16

A study in concentration and determination, Charlie regarded himself as the fittest player on the staff when he arrived at Aston Villa as a teenager in the late 1950s and believed the same thing to be true at the time of his departure from the club, at the age of 34, in 1976.

Aston Villa's ongoing love affair with the League Cup continued in March 1975 when a team captained by Ian Ross (left) and spearheaded by striker Ian "Chico" Hamilton defeated Norwich City 1-0 at Wembley Stadium, thanks to a Ray Graydon goal, scored on the rebound after Kevin Keelan, the Norwich goalkeeper, had tipped Graydon's penalty-kick against the post. This was the triumph that truly kick-started the successes of the Ron Saunders era and in the following month Villa would secure the promotion from the Second Division that saw them back in top-flight football for the first time in eight years.

Brian Little attempts to squeeze past David Stringer of Norwich City during the 1975 League Cup final at Wembley.

# Savouring Success

Ray Graydon, the sole goalscorer in the 1975 League Cup final, hugs Ron Saunders in celebration after the final whistle had gone in the match to give Villa their first major trophy since they had won the same competition for the first time in 1961. The joyfulness of the occasion was such that even Ron, a man not often given to public displays of emotion, had little choice but to join in with the fun.

# A Hasty Exit

Dennis Mortimer and Frank Carrodus of Aston Villa, together with Johnny Hamilton and Stewart Kennedy of Rangers, dash for the safety of the dressing rooms when a "friendly" match in October 1976 is abandoned in the 53rd minute after drunken Rangers supporters had invaded the pitch and play had been stopped. Some 99 arrests were made and 35 people hospitalized.

# The **1977** League Cup Final

John Deehan, the young Aston Villa striker, has a header at goal during the League Cup final with Everton at Wembley in the spring of 1977. Ken McNaught, the Everton centre-back, pictured here, would join Villa for a £200,000 record transfer fee in the summer of that year. Andy Gray peers over McNaught's shoulder but neither he nor Deehan nor anyone else was successful in scoring during a desperately dull final that ended 0-0.

The combined efforts of Leighton Phillips, John Burridge, Chris Nicholl and John Gidman cannot prevent Mick Lyons equalizing for Everton in the second replay of the 1977 League Cup final, at Old Trafford, making the score 2-2 and sending the match into extra-time.

# The Final Act

Brian Little prods the ball past David Lawson, the Everton goalkeeper, for the winning goal, two minutes from the end of extra-time, in Aston Villa's 3-2 victory over Everton in the League Cup final at Old Trafford in 1977. This was the third time Villa had lifted the trophy, and their fifth final. Little would describe the goal as "probably the simplest in my career". The final went on to a second replay after the goalless draw at Wembley in the first match had been followed by a 1-1 draw at Hillsborough.

# Solid Silver

RIGHT: Aston Villa captain Chris Nicholl shows off the League Cup, won at Old Trafford after the marathon slog against Everton in the spring of 1977.

# –LEGENDS–

## Brian Little

Youthful promise can often be deceptive in football. Many a lauded youngster has found the ascent from youth level to the first team to be a step too far. It was not so with Brian Little. Part of the side that won both the FA Youth Cup and the Dusseldorf International Youth Tournament in 1972, Brian was co-opted into the first team that same season and made the switch seamlessly, scoring once and setting up two of the other goals in a 5-1 victory over Torquay United that saw Villa clinch the Third Division title in front of a 38,000 Villa Park crowd.

Brian could appear languid on the field of play, but that was due only to his thoughtful, considered style. One of his key traits was to go, unselfishly, wide and play neat, natty through-balls for more direct striking partners, most effectively, from the mid-1970s onwards, and to explosive effect, for Andy Gray. His crossing was exceptional too and he was, of course, a fine finisher of chances when they fell to him. The cartilage trouble that would end his career first came notably to the fore in the 1975/6 season and it was most unfortunate that he played his final game of football, away to Manchester United, aged only 28, in the spring of 1980.

Brian Little shoots for goal during the 1975 League Cup final with Norwich City, in his third season as a first-team regular.

> *Brian Little was a world-class player. He was brilliant at running across the back four. He'd watch your foot come back then go with perfect timing.*
>
> Charlie Aitken

ABOVE: A final flourish and the ball slips pleasingly into the Everton net for the winner as Little's last-ditch goal wins Aston Villa the League Cup in the spring of 1977.

BELOW: Little (right) enjoys the aftermath of the victory against Everton as he helps parade the League Cup trophy alongside Gordon Smith (left) and Chris Nicholl (centre).

## FOOTBALL -STATS-

### Brian Little

Name: Brian Little

Born: 1953

Playing Career: 1971-1980

Clubs: Aston Villa

Aston Villa Appearances: 301

Aston Villa Goals: 82

England Appearances: 1

Goals: 0

Managerial Career: 1989-

Clubs: Darlington, Leicester City, Aston Villa, Stoke City, West Bromwich Albion, Hull City, Tranmere Rovers, Wrexham, Gainsborough Trinity

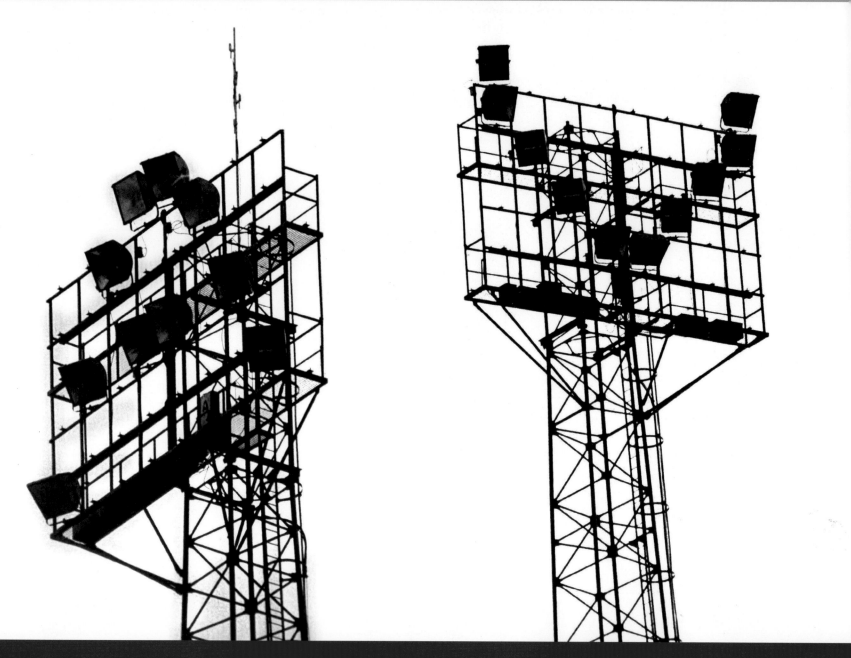

# Spelling Things Out

ABOVE: The floodlights that were unveiled at Villa Park in 1971, with the initials A and V spelled out in the bulbs, helped make the ground even more distinctive.

OPPOSITE: It appears as though Jimmy Rimmer, the goalkeeper newly signed by Villa from Arsenal in the summer of 1977, could be being dismissed on his debut for the club at Queen's Park Rangers in August of that year. Despite the referee's dramatic stance, this was actually only a booking for Rimmer after he had committed the offence of marking the turf inside the penalty area. Rimmer would make the goalkeeping position at Villa almost entirely his own for the next five years.

# Through Rain and Shine

Ken McNaught (centre), the Aston Villa centre-back, battles for the ball with Arsenal players Alan Hudson (left) and Malcolm MacDonald, during a match at Highbury in February 1978. McNaught would, from the end of that season, form a near indomitable partnership in Villa's central defence with Allan Evans, an equally rugged fellow Scot, who had, like McNaught, also been signed in 1977, as a striker, from Dunfermline Athletic. They would form the bedrock of Villa's subsequent, hugely successful half-decade.

Ken McNaught keeps his eye on the ball at muddy, rainy Highbury as Malcolm MacDonald seeks to gain the advantage. Villa would emerge 1-0 victors in this match, thanks to an own goal from MacDonald.

# –LEGENDS–

## Andy Gray

There was always a degree of pzazz about Andy Gray, a confidence, on and off the pitch, that set him apart as the striker lit up Villa Park during the second half of the 1970s. Three goals from Gray in the autumn of 1976, in a 5-2 victory over Ipswich Town, marked the first hat-trick from a Villa player in the top flight for a decade and took the club top of the league. It was the type of timing that ensured that Gray, who had arrived from Dundee United for a £110,000 fee in 1975, would become talismanic of Villa's revival after almost a decade trawling the depths of the lower divisions.

A prize goalscorer, most especially in the air, clever, sharp and quick, Gray established himself as a high-calibre striker not only through regularly putting the ball in the net but because he did so with real aplomb. He had become, by the late 1970s, one of the most valued talents in the British game, and in 1977, aged 22, was named both the Professional Footballers' Association Player of the Year and Young Player of the Year, the first individual to achieve the double award. Injury disrupted his progress at Villa – he needed three cartilage operations in early 1979 alone – and, having chafed against Ron Saunders' abrasive management style, Gray was confined by the manager to the reserves for the start of the 1979/80 season. He was soon moved on to Wolverhampton Wanderers for a British record fee of £1,469,000. A second spell at Villa in the mid-1980s was less successful, but could not erase the powerful impact Gray had made on the club in his prime.

Andy Gray in the summer of 1978, when he was, uniquely, the holder of both the Professional Footballers' Association Young Player of the Year and Player of the Year titles.

> *What I wanted to do most of all was score a goal.*
>
> Andy Gray on his approach to playing football

## FOOTBALL -STATS-

### Andy Gray

Name: Andrew Mullen Gray

Born: 1955

Playing Career: 1973-1990

Clubs: Dundee United, Aston Villa, Wolverhampton Wanderers, Everton, Aston Villa, West Bromwich Albion, Rangers, Cheltenham Town

Aston Villa Appearances: 208

Aston Villa Goals: 78

Scotland Appearances: 20

Goals: 6

ABOVE: An unusual sighting of Andy Gray working back in defence. Here he is helping John Burridge (Villa goalkeeper) and Chris Nicholl (centre-back) to clear from Mick Lyons of Everton at Goodison Park in August 1976.

RIGHT: Andy Gray at his best, causing mayhem in an opposing defence, this time that of Everton during the 1977 League Cup final at Wembley. Gray, in the early 1980s, would join Everton and help that club to land the League Championship title and the European Cup Winners' Cup.

*Europe's Best*

# 1980-1982

“

*We won it and no one can take that away from us.*

Gordon Cowans on Villa's European Cup triumph

”

Peter Withe leaps exuberantly after scoring the only goal of the 1982 European Cup final for Aston Villa against Bayern Munich.

There was an energy and vitality about the Aston Villa team of the early 1980s that was utterly irresistible. Not only did they play a style of football that was based appealingly on highly refined skill, but they did so at a tempo that has rarely been seen in the British game. Watching Villa in full flow during that era was to see one of the great spectacles that football has delivered in this country.

A classic Aston Villa goal of the 1980s would begin deep in the team's own half, but rarely was the build-up cautious and deliberate. Instead, the ball would be whipped forward with startling efficiency, through the players' uncanny close control, with the chance being finished off in emphatic style. This was a team that rarely scored scrappy goals. It was an approach to the game incredibly difficult to hone, to get right, relying as it did on players fulfilling their roles not only to the highest standard but unerringly quickly as soon as the ball was delivered to them, and it was the speed of execution of this high-grade football that caught so many opponents on the hop. That Villa maintained such a demandingly high level of football throughout their peak period from 1980 to 1982, when they landed not only the Football League Championship title but also the European Cup, is a tribute to the combination of the assiduous management of Ron Saunders and the players' professionalism and receptiveness to Saunders' ideas.

This is a team that has mysteriously never been given its full due for its achievements; a team with excellent technical players such as Gordon Cowans, Tony Morley, Des Bremner and Dennis Mortimer; intelligent, crafty strikers in Peter Withe and Gary Shaw; fine goalkeepers in Jimmy Rimmer and Nigel Spink; and excellent defenders such as Kenny Swain, Gary Williams, Allan Evans, Ken McNaught and Colin Gibson, all of whom had the ability to augment attacks to great effect. Those who played less often, such as David Geddis, tended to match the magnificence of their team-mates as and when they did come in to the team.

This was a football team fit to match any opponent they faced, as they showed in eliminating European opposition of the highest calibre to claim, at the first time of asking, the European Cup, during the 1981/2 season, a triumph that puts the club in that elite band of five British clubs to have won the trophy and which deservedly set Aston Villa forever among the great names of modern European football.

Thousands of expectant Aston Villa supporters cram into Arsenal's Highbury Stadium on the last day of the 1980/1 season in the hope of seeing their club land the championship. Here Ken McNaught spearheads an aerial Villa attack.

## Ron Saunders

It seemed most odd when Ron Saunders once compared his Aston Villa players to the stars of showbiz. This, after all, was a manager who always set his face against making any kind of song and dance over the game of football. That forced comparison came from him in defence of his players after revelations that they were on win bonuses that drew comparison with other spheres of popular entertainment and Saunders defended his men by stating that they worked hard for every penny they earned in entertaining sumptuously their public to the same level as other artistes.

Saunders' Villa teams entertained in style, and the tightly constructed framework that enabled them to display their talents to the full was put in place by one of the most demanding managers the British game has ever known. Before any other consideration, Saunders ensured that his players were commando fit and that they adhered strictly to his disciplinary demands. Anyone who failed him, in any way, was mercilessly excluded from his plans. He took control of Villa in the summer of 1974 and transformed a club that was struggling to escape the confines of the Second Division into one that, eight years later, would be the best team in Europe. He did it in style too, transforming Villa into a team in which every component would work to perfection like a beautiful machine to overwhelm less well-drilled opponents. It may have matched showbiz for entertainment value, but the team that Saunders moulded proved to be one of the purest exponents of football that the British game has seen.

> "His ways were probably a lot more beneficial to us than if we'd had a manager who was a lot easier on us. He built three sides in the time he was at Villa and I've got nothing but admiration for him."
>
> Gordon Cowans

Ron Saunders in January 1975, during the manager's initial, explosively successful, season with Aston Villa, during which the club won the League Cup, together with promotion back to the top level of English football for the first time after almost a decade away.

ABOVE: A hands-on manager, Ron Saunders takes to the field to oversee the treatment being given to the injured Ken McNaught during Villa's home win over Manchester City in January 1981. Jimmy Rimmer, Dennis Mortimer, Kenny Swain and Des Bremner also hover around.

RIGHT: Ron Saunders looks suitably unemotional as he lifts the League Cup after Villa's 1977 triumph over Everton at Old Trafford.

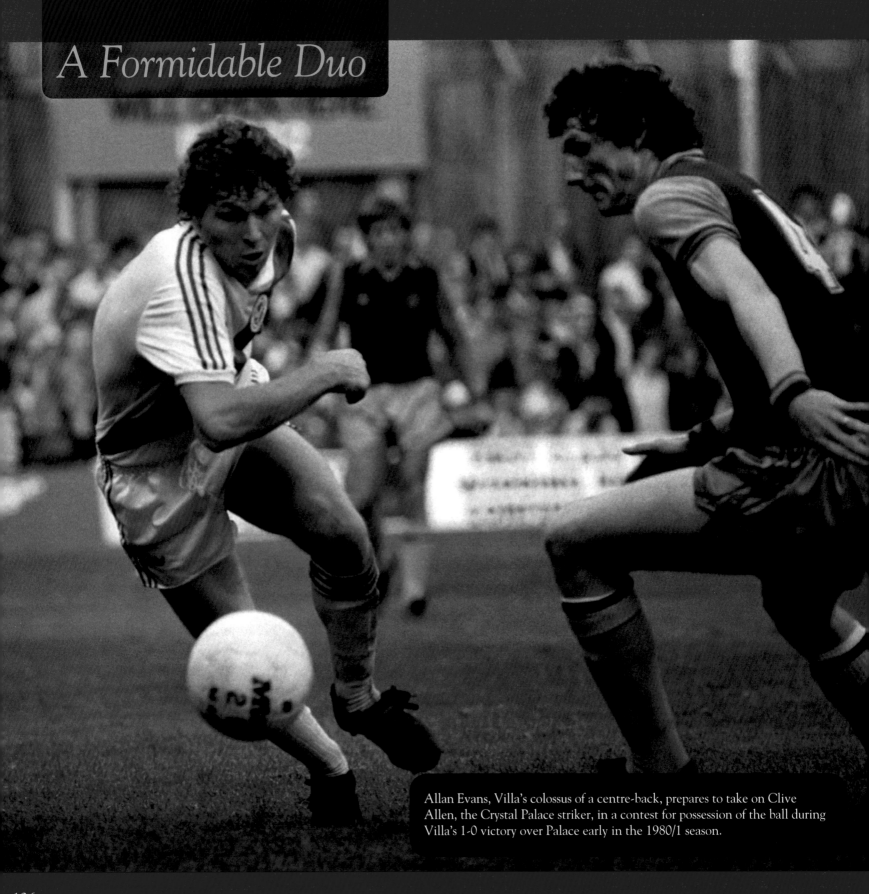

# A Formidable Duo

Allan Evans, Villa's colossus of a centre-back, prepares to take on Clive Allen, the Crystal Palace striker, in a contest for possession of the ball during Villa's 1-0 victory over Palace early in the 1980/1 season.

Ken McNaught, Evans' steady defensive partner, proves equally unyielding in dealing with Allen in the same game.

The Centre of Attention

Ken McNaught wins a header against Frank Worthington, the Birmingham City striker, in front of a busy tableau of supporters banked up behind the players during the Second City derby at St Andrews in October 1980. Villa emerged as 2-1 winners.

# Teamwork

The team spirit is evident as a tight-knit bunch of Villa players descend on Gordon Cowans to congratulate him on scoring the opening goal in the autumn 1980 win over Birmingham City.

Much of the game seems to have been played with their heads.

LEFT: Ipswich Town emerged as Aston Villa's most prominent rivals for the league title during the 1980/1 season. The clubs also met in the FA Cup in early January 1981 and here, in that Cup tie at Portman Road, Peter Withe indulges in a friendly tussle with Terry Butcher, the Ipswich centre-back.

BELOW: Another joust between Butcher and Withe concludes in a tangle of arms and legs. The Cup encounter would result in a 1-0 defeat for Villa and during the early months of 1981 the two clubs would be involved in a tussle at the top of the league that was just as tight as that Cup tie had been. The lead changed hands several times throughout the season, most notably in the concluding segment of the campaign.

# –LEGENDS–

## Tony Morley

Inconsistency and injury made Tony Morley's first season at Aston Villa a disappointing one after he had signed from Burnley for £200,000 in the summer of 1979. The transformation in the player after that initial year proved one of the most dramatic for any individual in Villa's history. He had been tried on both wings and as striker during that first season, but in 1980/1 he became established as Villa's wide-left midfield player, a position in which his speed, inventiveness and quick-thinking were complemented by a dozen goals that made him the club's third-highest goalscorer during the championship-winning season.

It had taken Morley longer than others to come to terms with Ron Saunders' demands. Morley was a player of style and wit, with magnificent ability, and for such an individual the manager's demand that all of his players work tirelessly back and forth would be one that Morley could grow into only gradually. When he did, both he and Villa were rewarded spectacularly. This was a player who had two great feet, who was a fine crosser and distributor of the ball, with incredibly fast reactions and who scored goals that few others could match. The leading scorer in Villa's European Cup campaign in 1982, his twisting run to set up Peter Withe's winning goal in the final was the type of thing that was mere routine brilliance for Morley.

Swift and sharp, Tony Morley's deftness and invention on the wing made him an invaluable asset to Villa during the club's successes of the early 1980s.

> "
> *He had fantastic ability and was probably our matchwinner. On his day he could turn things around and create things for us.*
>
> Gordon Cowans on Tony Morley
> "

ABOVE: The elusive Tony Morley dashes between Ian Bowyer and Kenny Swain, a one-time Villa team-mate, during a 2-1 Villa win over Nottingham Forest at the City Ground in February 1983.

## FOOTBALL
# – STATS –

## Tony Morley

**Name:** William Anthony Morley

**Born:** 1954

**Playing Career:** 1972-1990

**Clubs:** Preston North End, Burnley, Aston Villa, West Bromwich Albion, Seiko, Den Haag, West Bromwich Albion, Tampa Bay Rowdies, Hamrun Spartans

**Aston Villa Appearances:** 180

**Aston Villa Goals:** 34

**England Appearances:** 6

**Goals:** 0

The effort required to make his searing runs is expressed on Tony Morley's face as he prepares to drive at the Crystal Palace defence during a match in the autumn of 1980. Morley was one of seven Villa players who played in all 42 league matches during that championship-winning season, one in which the club used a mere 14 players in all in their efforts to clinch their first title for 71 years.

It is on grey, misty winter days that league titles can be won and lost. Des Bremner displays the gritty attitude that kept Villa on course to win the league during the 1980/1 season; with the Holte End looking over his shoulder, he stretches every sinew as he attempts to halt the forward progress of Paul Power of Manchester City in a match in late January 1981 that Villa won 1-0.

# Taut and Tense Occasions

A productive moment for Villa as Gordon Cowans slips home a penalty in a 3-1 win at Everton in February that maintained the team's momentum as the title race

The glaring contrast between victory and defeat is written in the expressions of Steve Archibald, the Tottenham Hotspur striker, and Gary Williams, the Aston Villa left-back, during Villa's 2-0 defeat at White Hart Lane in March 1981. This was the first time Villa had lost in the league for three months and it came only a week after the team had let slip a 2-0 lead over Manchester United at Villa Park to draw 3-3. This was a testing stage in Villa's tight, season-long contest with Ipswich Town for the First Division title.

# Seizing the Initiative

"

*The way we played on the day was phenomenal.*

Peter Withe on the 3-0 win over Middlesbrough in April 1981 that made Villa champions-elect

"

Peter Withe communes with the Villa Park crowd after heading the second goal in the 3-0 defeat of Middlesbrough that took Villa to the verge of becoming First Division champions in the spring of 1981. "We scored three but it could have been ten," Withe says of that match. "We just camped in their half."

This was Villa's penultimate fixture of the season and it left them four points clear of Ipswich Town, who had two matches to play, while Villa would travel to Arsenal on the final Saturday of the season. With two points awarded for a win, Villa was in a strong position to clinch the championship. Withe, the 29-year-old centre-forward who had won the First Division with Nottingham Forest in 1978, had been brought in from Newcastle United in the summer of 1980, Villa paying a club record fee of £500,000 for him. Withe's 20 league goals did much to fuel Villa's title challenge.

# D-Day

A crowd of 60,000 fits into every fragment of space at Highbury to watch Arsenal host budding champions Aston Villa on the first Saturday of May 1981. Here Allan Evans, the Villa centre-back, challenges Alan Sunderland, the Arsenal striker, in front of a vast bank of Villa supporters packed into Arsenal's Clock End.

Pelé appears on the pitch at half-time and breaks into a jog, to wild acclaim from the crowd.

A Villa fan still manages to have a cheery word with Jimmy Rimmer despite having been uplifted by the police.

Ron Saunders, the Villa manager, and his backroom staff endure a tense 90 minutes that conclude with Arsenal winning 2-0.

143

Villa fans begin their celebrations in Arsenal's Clock End after hearing that Ipswich Town are on the verge of a 2-1 defeat to Middlesbrough and that the title is about to be won by Villa.

The Villa players celebrate gustily in their Highbury dressing room after the match with Arsenal and their confirmation as League Champions.

# Titled Gentlemen

Dennis Mortimer, the Villa captain, and Ron Saunders, manager, relax and enjoy the moment in the Highbury dressing room after clinching the title. Both men had exuded, throughout the season, the type of resolve and determination essential to a title-winning team.

Outside, on the pitch, the good-humoured Villa fans' celebrations continue.

# —LEGENDS—

## Gordon Cowans

Gordon Cowans was an unerringly fine creative player for Aston Villa in three spells at the club over two decades. His calm, controlled approach to the game and his imaginative use of the ball was evident from the moment he made his debut as a 17-year-old in 1976 – and his role in the team was to use his refined skills to prompt good things out of others. He and the powerful, hard-running, hard-tackling Dennis Mortimer made for an indomitable duo in the centre of the Villa midfield during the late 1970s and early 1980s and they proved to be the pivotal force as Villa landed the league title and the European Cup.

The composure demonstrated by Cowans was essential to a team that relied on pace and sharpness – he could "sit" and ping passes of the highest accuracy to his speedy colleagues – and he was also invaluable in taking set-pieces. "Sid" was also, for all his splendid talents, a modest, unassuming individual, as popular for his pleasant personality as for his devastatingly deadly passing powers.

Gordon Cowans' expression after a 4-0 home victory over Tottenham Hotspur in October 1982 reflects the enormous pleasure he derived from playing the game of football so well.

> " *My ambition is to make a run that Sid doesn't read.* "
>
> David Platt, 1990

Cowans hurdles a challenge during a 2-0 defeat of Swansea City in September 1982.

## FOOTBALL -STATS-

### Gordon Cowans

Name: Gordon Sidney Cowans

Born: 1958

Playing Career: 1976-1997

Clubs: Aston Villa, Bari, Aston Villa, Blackburn Rovers, Aston Villa, Derby County, Wolverhampton Wanderers, Sheffield United, Bradford City, Stockport County, Burnley

Aston Villa Appearances: 527

Aston Villa Goals: 59

England Appearances: 10

Goals: 2

# Just Champion

RIGHT: Peter Withe challenges Bruce Grobbelaar, the Liverpool goalkeeper, in the air, at Anfield during a 0-0 draw in the autumn of 1981. Villa struggled, as champions, to match the consistency in the league that had won them the title. They would conclude the 1981/2 season in mid-table.

It's the second leg of the European Cup second-round tie between Aston Villa and Dynamo Berlin at Villa Park and Gordon Cowans, in splendid isolation, looks sure to score. But Cowans and Villa were to draw a blank on the night and lose 1-0 to the East German champions, who soaked up a great deal of pressure and took the lead after quarter of an hour thanks to Frank Terletzki. This left the tie poised beautifully at 2-2, but with no further scoring on the night, Villa went through to the quarter-finals, having scored two away goals to the East Germans' one.

LEFT: Jimmy Rimmer, the Aston Villa goalkeeper, looking dazed and confused, is given treatment during a match with Manchester City at Maine Road in December 1981. Rimmer had been with Manchester United when they had won the European Cup in 1968 but had been reserve to Alex Stepney. He would be an ever-present for Villa in the league and cup competitions in the 1981/2 season and would start in the European Cup final in Rotterdam only to suffer the disappointment of having to leave the field with only nine minutes played due to a recurrence of the neck injury he had sustained in the final league match of the season.

# Euro Experts

Goals from Gary Shaw and Ken McNaught gave Villa the 2-0 victory over Dynamo Kiev in March 1982 that sent the club into the semi-finals of the European Cup. Shaw's opener, a finish from a tight angle after a neat exchange of passes with Gordon Cowans, arrived after only five minutes. McNaught's powerful header, from Cowans' corner, came shortly before half-time.

"*Once we got past Dynamo Kiev we thought we could go all the way.*

Gordon Cowans on Villa's European Cup run

"

# Striking Gold

Peter Withe sends several Bayern Munich defenders in the opposite direction as he cuts through the West German team's defence to fire in a shot that curled wide of goal during the first half of the 1982 European Cup final.

Tony Morley gets the Bayern defence in a twist during the Rotterdam final.

Nigel Spink parries a fierce 15-yard shot from Karl-Heinz Rummenigge in front of the Villa supporters during the first half of the European Cup final in Rotterdam's De Kuip Stadium. Rummenigge had twice been named European Footballer of the Year by 1982 – Spink was playing only his second game for Villa since his debut on Boxing Day in 1979. He had replaced the injured Jimmy Rimmer early on in the final. One Villa banner behind the goal teases the Germans with the slogan "1918 1945 1966 And Now 82 It's Just Not Your Century". So late 20th century – so politically incorrect.

# The Final Reckoning

LEFT: Tony Morley's trickery on the left wing was a problem for the Bayern defence almost from the kick-off. Here he is the victim of a desperate and clumsy attempt from Wolfgang Dremmler to halt his progress.

BELOW: Villa players converge on the grounded Peter Withe to congratulate him on his 67th-minute goal in the final. The striker's fellow celebrants are, from left: Des Bremner, Tony Morley, Gordon Cowans, Kenny Swain (partially hidden), Gary Williams and Gary Shaw. Bayern Munich were about to suffer the first defeat in a Cup final of any sort in their long and illustrious history.

LEFT: Captain Dennis Mortimer becomes the first Villa player to lift the European Cup, at the conclusion of a tumultuous, momentous night in Rotterdam.

Gordon Cowans is crowned a European champion with the great trophy itself after the victory over Bayern Munich. Tony Morley (left) and Pat Heard help him to balance the outsize bauble atop his head.

> " *This Aston Villa team does not play English football as we know it; it is a team with a much more modern European-style of football than the other English teams.* "
>
> Paul Breitner, captain of Bayern Munich, May 1982

Members of the Aston Villa squad who landed the European Cup celebrate their momentous victory in the aftermath of the win over Bayern Munich in Rotterdam's De Kuip Stadium. The players are, back row, left to right: Pat Heard, Andy Blair, Colin Gibson, Gary Shaw, Ken McNaught, Jimmy Rimmer, Des Bremner, David Geddis. Front row, left to right: Gordon Cowans, Allan Evans, Dennis Mortimer, Kenny Swain, Tony Morley.

Peter Withe and Nigel Spink show how much claiming the European Cup means to them by giving it a long, lingering kiss.

ABOVE: Tony Barton gets a low-down view of the match with Arsenal from the Highbury dugout in 1982. Barton had been assistant to Ron Saunders and took over when Saunders quit suddenly after a disagreement with the Board of Directors in February of that year.

RIGHT: Tony Barton was confirmed as permanent Villa manager in April 1982. A man with a pleasant way about him, his first major task was merely to ensure that Villa won the European Cup.

173

# –LEGENDS–

## Peter Withe

It was the persuasive powers of Ron Saunders that convinced Peter Withe that he ought to join Aston Villa in the summer of 1980 rather than the clutch of other clubs pursuing the striker. "He wanted you to perform to the very best of your ability in every game rather than in every three or four games," Withe said in praise of his new manager. That clinched the signing of a player whose own self-motivation throughout his career was always to push himself to the utmost.

At the beginning of the 1980/1 season, Withe put money on Villa winning the League Cup and winning the FA Cup but not on his new club winning the league title because the odds on that were too short. Perhaps the bookmakers had, in common with Saunders, decided that the addition of Withe now made Villa the complete championship-winning side. A magnificent leader of the line, Withe not only scored regularly and efficiently but created numerous other goals, particularly through his power in the air and his highly accurate knock-downs to inrushing midfield players or to striking partners such as Gary Shaw. Few players have made a stronger and more immediate impact on Villa throughout the club's history: without Withe, Villa's chances of landing the league title and the European Cup would have been diminished considerably.

Peter Withe was not only an excellent player but a fine communicator, with the confidence and ability to motivate and inspire his team-mates.

> *We'd always lacked a true out-and-out centre-forward – a man we could rely on to be in the box and do that job for us. Peter did the job perfectly.*
>
> Dennis Mortimer on the impact made on the Villa team by the signing of Peter Withe

## FOOTBALL
## –STATS–

### Peter Withe

Name: Peter Withe

Born: 1951

Playing Career: 1971-1990

Clubs: Southport, Barrow, Port Elizabeth City, Arcadia Shepherds, Wolverhampton Wanderers, Portland Timbers, Birmingham City, Nottingham Forest, Newcastle United, Aston Villa, Sheffield United, Huddersfield Town

Aston Villa Appearances: 233

Aston Villa Goals: 92

England Appearances: 11

Goals: 1

Managerial Career: 1991-2007

Clubs: Wimbledon, Thailand and Indonesia

ABOVE: Peter Withe was never less than fully committed to his task of leading the line for Aston Villa, as here in a match with Manchester City in 1982.

BELOW: A frequent sight in the first half of the 1980s – Peter Withe turning away in celebration of one of his goals, this time against Everton at Goodison Park.

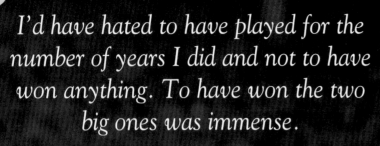

> *I'd have hated to have played for the number of years I did and not to have won anything. To have won the two big ones was immense.*
>
> Dennis Mortimer

## FOOTBALL
# –STATS–

### Dennis Mortimer

Name: Dennis Mortimer

Born: 1952

Playing Career: 1969-1987

Clubs: Coventry City, Aston Villa, Brighton & Hove Albion, Birmingham City

Aston Villa Appearances: 406

Aston Villa Goals: 36

Drive and determination, combined with supreme athleticism, made Dennis Mortimer an inspirational captain for Aston Villa during their greatest era. Here he hurdles Gary Stevens, the Everton full-back, during a 2-0 Villa Park victory in February 1983.

# –LEGENDS–

## Dennis Mortimer

One of the indelible images of Aston Villa in the early 1980s is of Dennis Mortimer streaking through on goal from midfield before planting the ball expertly behind an opposing goalkeeper. The team captain and the driving force in the Villa midfield, Dennis scored one such goal in January 1981 to seal a 2-0 home victory over Liverpool that he believed at the time was likely to finish off Liverpool as contenders for the title that season. It was a delicious moment for Mortimer, a Liverpudlian, especially as his hunch proved to be correct. It seemed equally significant that when the final whistle blew at Highbury on 2nd May 1981 to signify that Villa had won the league title, Mortimer, always available to take the ball, should have been the man in possession at that moment.

It was at Christmas 1975 that Dennis Mortimer was signed for the significantly high fee of £175,000 from Coventry City. A press call saw him covered in Christmas gift wrap at the behest of the snappers who thought it a jolly wheeze to make him out to be a present to the Villa fans. A decade of superb service was to follow, and Mortimer, who admitted he knew little about the club on his arrival, became one of the greatest players ever to don the Villa shirt.

Nicely poised and balanced, Dennis Mortimer eases the ball away from Howard Gayle of Birmingham City during Villa's 1-0 derby win in April 1983.

LEFT: Villa's inspirational captain rises above Kenny Dalglish of Liverpool to win the ball during a match at Villa Park in 1982.

RIGHT: Dennis is once again at the heart of the action as he contests a midfield battle with Franz Thijssen of Ipswich Town in January 1981.

Policemen, photographers, journalists and club directors were among the few to be allowed to witness Villa's first match in defence of the European Cup they had won in the spring of 1982. Crowd trouble in Brussels during the semi-final between Anderlecht and Villa had led UEFA to ban spectators from Villa's next home match in Europe, which proved to be an encounter with Besiktas, the champions of Turkey.

BELOW: Tony Morley shoots at goal during the match against Besiktas. A 3-1 victory set up Villa nicely for the return in Istanbul and a 0-0 draw there saw Villa ease into the second round.

# A Shaw Thing

Gary Shaw, Villa's exciting young striker of the early 1980s, rounds Alex Williams, Manchester City goalkeeper, to score the only goal of the game in a league fixture at Maine Road in September 1982. A teenager when he broke into the Villa team, Shaw's neatness and nippiness around the penalty area promised much and he would finish the 1982/3 season as the club's leading goalscorer, with 26 in all competitions. Sadly, that would prove to be the peak season for him in terms of goals scored, since injuries hit him hard and although he remained a Villa player for most of the rest of the 1980s, a series of six knee operations drastically curtailed his career.

# –LEGENDS–

## Des Bremner

In a team of unsung heroes, Des Bremner was the Villa player given the least fanfare of all, although this unassuming Highlander would probably not have had it any other way. In a team that worked hard, chivvied opponents into errors and chased rigorously after the ball, Des Bremner was invaluable since all those elements of football were a natural part of his game.

A non-glamorous role suited Des perfectly, enabling him to get on with a mountain of work in each game as he manoeuvred tirelessly in to out as a right-sided midfield player, varying his role by darting up the wing, getting crosses in, getting on the end of crosses and occasionally popping up with a goal. He may have gone largely unnoticed by the public, but his popularity with his team-mates was in inverse proportion to that near anonymity. To those who played alongside him he was never anything other than a star.

> *Des Bremner was absolutely fabulous, probably the most important member of the side.*
>
> Gordon Cowans

The unselfish running of Des Bremner was vital to all of Villa's momentous successes during the 1980s.

With his flawless concentration and determination, Des prepares to get an effort in on goal in a match with Nottingham Forest.

## Des Bremner

Name: Desmond George Bremner

Born: 1952

Playing Career: 1972-1994

Clubs: Hibernian, Aston Villa, Birmingham City, Fulham, Walsall, Stafford Rangers, Sutton Town

Aston Villa Appearances: 227

Aston Villa Goals: 10

Scotland Appearances: 1

Goals: 0

LEFT: Des Bremner keeps his eye on the ball as he prepares to challenge Frank Stapleton of Manchester United for possession, in front of a packed Trinity Road Stand.

BELOW: Des streaks away from Paul Breitner, the Bayern Munich captain, during the 1982 European Cup final, in which Bremner excelled.

# A Return Journey

Villa, as European Cup holders, defended their trophy with vigour during the 1982/3 season. After defeating Besiktas, they eliminated Dinamo Bucharest of Romania in the second round. Here Gary Shaw celebrates the first goal of the hat-trick he contributed to Villa's 4-2 victory in the second leg, at Villa Park. A quarter-final defeat to Juventus, a side sprinkled with players who had won the World Cup for Italy the previous summer, concluded Villa's sparkling two-season odyssey in the European Cup.

Villa remained a potent power during the 1982/3 season and here goalkeeper Jimmy Rimmer makes a spectacular stop from Remi Moses, the Manchester United midfield player, during Villa's 2-1 victory at Villa Park in November 1982. The team that season almost picked itself, as in 1980/1, and the core of the league and European Cup winning side remained intact. But for a disastrous start, when Villa shipped nine goals in losing their opening three league games, they might have been serious title contenders. That was despite competing in six competitions that season, in which they won the European Super Cup, lost the World Clubs Cup final in Japan and reached the quarter-finals of the European Cup. They still finished sixth in the league, made the quarter-finals of the FA Cup and qualified for the 1983/4 UEFA Cup.

*Extreme Experiences*
# 1983-1992

Joy registers on the face of Allan Evans as the grounded Ken McNaught's diving header enters the Barcelona net to give Villa a 3-0 victory at Villa Park in January 1983 to clinch the European Super Cup.

*I played in many impressive stadiums in my career but few matched Villa Park for grandeur and atmosphere.*

Dennis Mortimer

**1983** A 3-1 aggregate victory over Barcelona sees Villa begin the new year by winning the European Super Cup. **1984** Tony Barton is dismissed and replaced as manager by Graham Turner, a 36-year-old who had previously been manager of Shrewsbury Town. Didier Six, a France international, becomes the first continental player to appear in Villa's first team. **1986** With Villa bottom of the First Division, Graham Turner is replaced by Billy McNeill, who arrives from Manchester City. **1987** Relegation to the Second Division sees Billy McNeill leave the club after only eight months to make way for Graham Taylor. **1988** On the final day of the season, a 0-0 draw at Swindon Town sends Villa back into the top flight. **1989** Ten days after Villa's final match of the 1988/9 season, a 5-1 defeat for West Ham United at Liverpool sees the London club relegated rather than Villa. **1990** A club record £1.5 million fee brings striker Tony Cascarino to Villa from Millwall; but Cascarino scores only twice in 10 games, despite Villa looking to him for goals as they chase the league title. A year after avoiding relegation on the final day of the season, Villa finish as runners-up to Liverpool, the League Champions. Doctor Jozef Venglos, a Slovakian, becomes Aston Villa manager in succession to Graham Taylor, who leaves Villa to become England manager after the World Cup. **1991** Once again, Villa only narrowly escape relegation, following a disastrous second half of the season. David Platt leaves for Bari in a £5.5 million deal that makes him the most expensive player to be transferred by Aston Villa. Doctor Venglos is dismissed as Villa manager after only one season and is replaced by Ron Atkinson. **1992** Ron Atkinson breaks the Villa transfer record for the third time in a year when he signs Dean Saunders, a striker, from Liverpool for £2.3 million.

Tony Daley, the locally born winger was the brightest and most exciting of the new talents that provided Aston Villa with inspiration as the club entered the 1990s.

Ken McNaught, the Aston Villa centre-back, makes a terrific tackle to block Kenny Dalglish's effort on goal in the 1-1 draw at Anfield in May 1983. This would be McNaught's penultimate match for Villa, only a year after he had helped the club win the European Cup. Kenny Swain had already departed, early in that season, and Tony Morley would leave for West Bromwich Albion later in 1983 as the team that conquered Europe was broken up with what appeared to be unseemly haste.

# Knocked for Six

Didier Six lies in a heap, as if being left behind by English football, during a match at Everton in October 1984, before looking rather groggy and disoriented as he awaits treatment for a knock. The France international, who had helped his country to win the European Championship in the summer of that year, had been signed, a week before the Everton match, on loan from Mulhouse. He was the first player from continental Europe to play for Villa but found it difficult to adjust his refined, technical style of play to the rough and tumble of the English game.

# Young Villans

Villa did have good young players coming through in the mid-1980s, such as Tony Dorigo (below), the Australian full-back, and Mark Walters (right), a Birmingham-born winger. Yet the transition between old and new had been far from smooth – several of the European Cup winning team had been jettisoned soon after that triumph and Villa, without their experience and know-how, had begun to flirt with relegation by the mid-1980s, before finally capitulating in 1987.

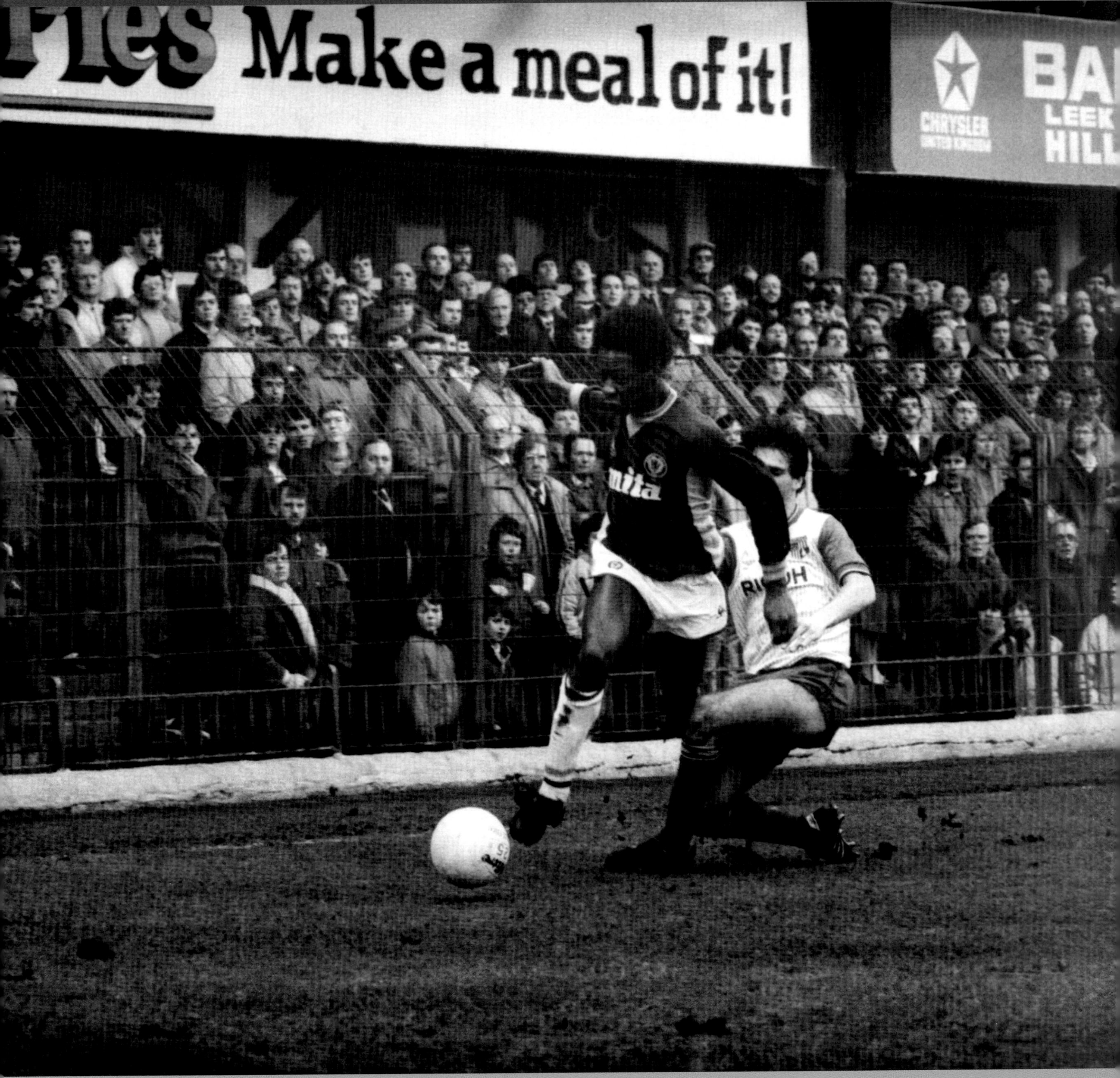
Make a meal of it!
CHRYSLER
UNITED KINGDOM
LEEK
HILL

Paul Elliott, the Aston Villa centre-back, demonstrates to perfection the art of tackling as he pursues, catches and dispossesses Kerry Dixon, the Chelsea striker, in a league fixture two days after Christmas 1986. Elliott, a personable individual whose social skills were as noticeable off the pitch as his abilities on it, was to earn a transfer, in the summer of 1987, to Pisa in the Italian League, at that time the most highly regarded strata of world football. By the early 1990s, Elliott would be back in Britain and plying his trade with Chelsea.

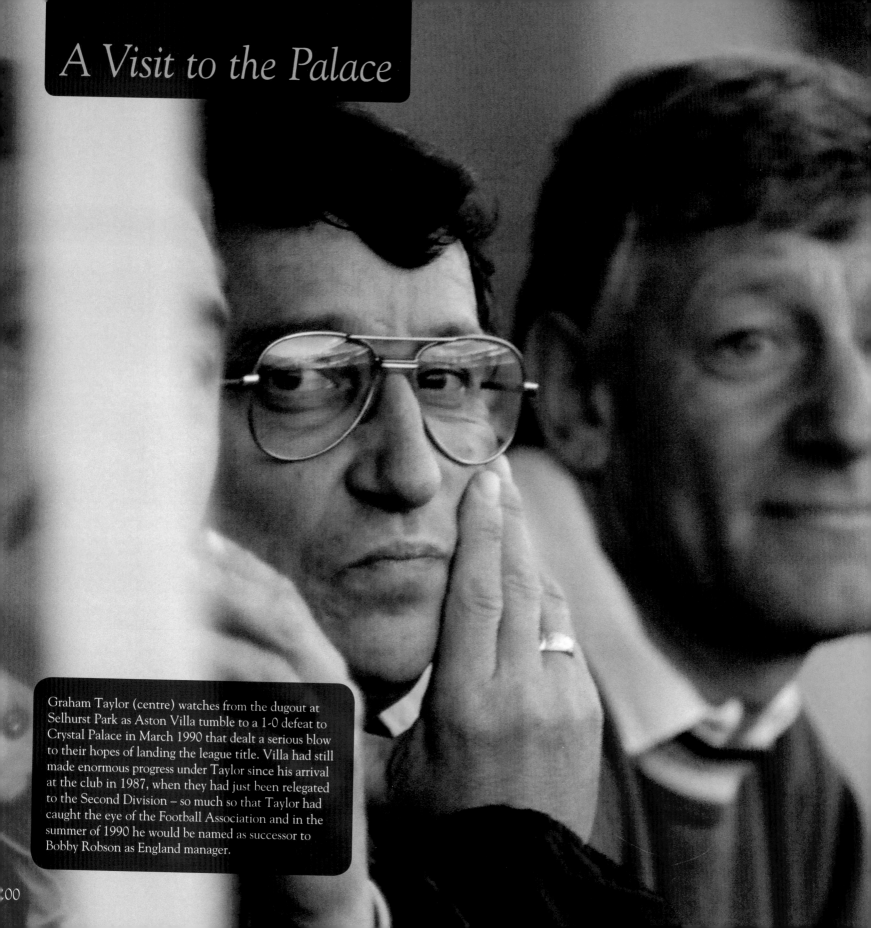

# A Visit to the Palace

Graham Taylor (centre) watches from the dugout at Selhurst Park as Aston Villa tumble to a 1-0 defeat to Crystal Palace in March 1990 that dealt a serious blow to their hopes of landing the league title. Villa had still made enormous progress under Taylor since his arrival at the club in 1987, when they had just been relegated to the Second Division – so much so that Taylor had caught the eye of the Football Association and in the summer of 1990 he would be named as successor to Bobby Robson as England manager.

Tony Cascarino (above) and David Platt (left) each struggle to get the better of Andy Thorn, the Palace centre-back, on a difficult afternoon for the Villa. The team had been top of the First Division for a month prior to this visit to South London, but this defeat saw them toppled from top spot and a series of indifferent performances from Villa in the remaining weeks of the season allowed Liverpool to claim the title.

# A Mersey Divide

ABOVE: Villa's final league match of the season, in the spring of 1990, took them to Goodison Park, where they participated in an enjoyable sunshine-strewn 3-3 draw with Everton. Here Nigel Spink, the Villa goalkeeper, combines with Kent Nielsen, the centre-back, to clear from Tony Cottee and Mike Newell, the Everton forwards, with Derek Mountfield (far left) and Paul McGrath, the other two Villa centre-backs, keeping guard. With strength in defence such as that, Villa looked sure to be able to build on a successful season that had seen them finish as runners-up after only their second year back in the top flight.

RIGHT: Chris Price, the Villa full-back, executes an all-or-nothing challenge on John Barnes, the Liverpool winger, at Anfield during Villa's first away league match of the 1990/1 season. Although Villa had challenged Liverpool strongly for the title the previous season, the team would lose this game 2-1 and would fall away in the first full season of the 1990s, only narrowly avoiding relegation in the spring of 1991.

# A Bright Spark

Tony Daley shows his usual balance, alacrity and style to ease away from a desperate challenge in a match with Norwich City in 1990. A wonderfully quick and entertaining winger with a knack for cutting inside at tremendous speed to score clever goals, Daley was hugely popular with the Villa support, but injuries were to hamper him during the first half of the 1990s in a sadly similar fashion to the way they had hampered the career development a decade earlier of Gary Shaw, another local boy who, like Daley, had come through the Villa youth system. It was most unfortunate that the club's best two local "finds" of the final two decades of the 20th century should suffer such a similar fate, but each still managed to leave many fine memories imprinted on the minds of Villa's followers.

# Intellectual Pursuits

Once again Aston Villa made British football history when, in July 1990, they appointed Doctor Jozef Venglos to replace Graham Taylor as manager. They thus became the first club in England's top division to enlist a manager whose origins were from outside the British Isles. Venglos, a cultured and amiable individual, a hugely experienced coach with a university doctorate in philosophy and physical education, and who could speak four languages, would become known inside Villa Park as "Gentleman Jo", but his advanced methods were too radical and refined to be accepted fully by the Villa playing staff, and he would remain at the club for only one season.

RIGHT: Doctor Venglos settles down to a game of chess in the autumn of 1990.

BELOW: Nigel Kennedy, the violinist, who achieved enormous popular success with the recording of his interpretation of Antonio Vivaldi's "The Four Seasons" in 1989, was pleased to disclose himself as a Villa supporter, happily marrying his love of the club with the usually more rarefied world of classical music.

The author would like to thank:
Richard Havers for his help as editor; Paul Moreton for the chance to put this book together; and David Scripps and Alex Waters at the *Daily Mirror* picture archive.

Special thanks to Dennis Mortimer